AND NOW FOR MY
43RD POINT

Giving the kiss of life to your sermon or talk

AND NOW FOR MY 43RD POINT

NICK & CLAIRE PAGE

Authentic

First published 2011 by Authentic Media Limited
52 Presley Way, Crownhill, Milton Keynes, Bucks, MK8 0ES

www.authenticmedia.co.uk

British Library Cataloguing in Publication Data
A catalogue record for this book is available from the British Library

ISBN: 978-1-85078-751-8

Book Design by Nick Page.
Cover Design by Phil Miles.
Printed and bound by CPI Group (UK) Ltd., Croydon, CR0 4YY.

This book is dedicated to our dearly departed Kenwood Brewmaster Coffee Maker, which gave its life so that this book might live

Greater love hath no small household appliance

Contents

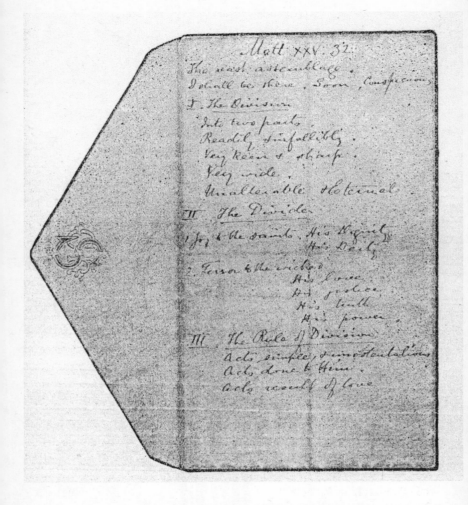

Spurgeon's preaching notes, for a sermon on Matt 25:32.
Yes, it really was 'back of an envelope' stuff.

Before we begin...

Nick: Let me welcome you to the book. I hope you enjoy reading it. It's not easy, two people writing a book together...

Claire: You mean 'Us'.

Nick: What?

Claire: You mean 'Let *us* welcome you to the book.'

Nick: Yes, but I'm the one writing this preface.

Claire: No, it's both of us.

Nick: Well I could have sworn I was the one tpying. Sorry, typing.

Claire: Check the names on the spine, chum. This isn't just your book.

Nick: Which is *exactly* what I was saying. It's not easy, two people writing a book together. And one of the biggest challenges we've had to face here is whether to write from the point of view of 'I' or 'We'.

Claire: I thought we'd agreed that it was going to be 'We'.

Nick: No, *you* agreed that. I was out of the room at the time. And in any case, in some places that just doesn't sound right.

Claire: But the reader's going to be confused if we keep changing it.

Nick: No, they're not – are you?

The Reader: What? Oh, er, sorry, I was nodding off then.

Nick: I was saying...

Claire: *We* were saying.

Nick: *We* were saying you might find it difficult to read this book if we mix our 'I's and our 'We's.

The Reader: Couldn't you just say 'Wii' instead?

Both: We thought of that, but there were trademark issues.

The Reader: Look, I really don't mind...

Nick: Good, because we decided that mostly we would say 'We'...

Claire: But sometimes we say 'I', when it's a personal anecdote...

Nick: Or when we forgot to change it.

The Reader: Fine. Whatever.

Both: Good. I'm glad we've made that clear.

Claire: Oh, and one more thing, we've set up a small website to accompany this book: www.43rdpoint.org.uk. It will have links to articles mentioned in the book, further resources and some extra material.

Nick: Although when you say 'we've' set this up, it's actually me.

Claire: Oh, do shut up.

AND NOW FOR MY 43rd POINT...

Sermon critically ill in hospital. Doctors say 'It's not long now.'

News has just reached us that Henry Sermon, for so long a fixture of the Sunday service, is fighting for his life.

He passed into a coma – much like many of his listeners – during a service at the tiny church of St Botolph the Underwhelmed, aged 1850. The official cause of illness has been given as irrelevance, leading to complete inertia.

'It came as a bit of a shock to us, I can tell you,' said one churchgoer. 'He had just got to the end of point 42 in his sermon on The Role of Dried Fruit in the Levitical Purity Code when he suddenly fell over and started emitting a thin, wheezing sound. We called the emergency services, who whisked him away to theological college.'

Widely Travelled

Henry Sermon was born in the Middle East, some time around the middle of the second century AD. His long and, at times, illustrious career has often been fraught with controversy. Widely travelled, he claims to have been to every part of the known world. Certainly, there isn't a major church or cathedral in the western world where Henry Sermon hasn't been heard.

One of his strengths has been his ability to cross divides. His

Henry Sermon in his usual preaching outfit.

friends and supporters have included not only Martin Luther, John Calvin and all the Reformers, but most of the Popes as well. In his glory years, such as the mid-nineteenth century, crowds of ten thousand people came to see him in action.

Struggling

Like anyone else, he has had his ups and downs. His role in nourishing the church and spreading the gospel has often been acclaimed, while his friends prefer to turn a blind eye to the part he played in launching the crusades. Nevertheless, he was in rude health up until relatively recently, but recent trends in communication and the decline in churchgoing have left him struggling, and over the past few decades there have been continuous rumours of his decline.

'You could see the old boy was struggling a bit,' said Heinz von Beanztin, Professor of Homiletics at the University of Badenbadenwurtemflugen-staffenberg. 'There were times when he would start to ramble and make no sense. Sometimes he would start off very brightly, but soon lose energy and forget where he was going. Latterly, indeed, he seemed to lose all sense of identity. It's been quite hard to watch his decline. And even harder to listen to it.'

In recent years, attempts have been made to inject new life into the old boy, with jabs of PowerPoint and frequent use of OHP.

But, if the latest news is correct, it will all be to no avail.

'I will be sad to see him go,' said Professor Beanztin, 'Not least because he always gave me an extra twenty minutes of sleep during the services.'

Preliminary Diagnosis

The Sermon R.I.P.

There's just one question facing the sermon today. Is it dead?

'Don't be stupid!' say its supporters. 'How can something so fundamental to the life of the Church be dead? Every week, in thousands of churches, the faithful hear a sermon, as they have for centuries. Sure, there are a few local difficulties, but there's no problem with the form itself.'

'Get real!' cry its detractors. 'Society's changed. It's a different world. The ways we learn, the ways we communicate, have been transformed in the past few decades. People are no longer going just to sit and listen to authority figures. They want to have their say.'

So who's right? What is the state of the sermon? Has it finally expired in the 21st century, or is there life in the old dog yet?

It has to be said that in recent years the voices of dissent do seem to be getting louder. And that dissent comes not just from fringe Christians, nor from social churchgoers: the complaints come from the heart of the Church. Emerging church publications and blogs sound the note of dissatisfaction felt by many at a form that to others is pivotal. People openly question the need for a sermon. Preaching books are still poured out, but many of them adopt a notably defensive tone, as if their authors realise, deep down, the game might finally be up. Even its supporters seem to recognise that the sermon is struggling. The preachers have trouble knowing who they're talking to, and the listeners have trouble remembering what they've been told.

Most of all, church attendance is declining. The Church is haemorrhaging people. There are many reasons why people leave church, but there is no doubt that boredom is one of them.

In the course of preparing this book, we asked hundreds of ordinary churchgoers about their experience of sermons. Their comments will be sprinkled throughout this book. But here are a few to start with:

> Sermons are too complicated: too much history, too long, too miserable.

> It's boring having the same people saying the same thing each week.

> We have lost our congregation. We need to change, relate to another generation.

> At least when the sermon starts you know you're on the last leg.

And those were some of the nicer ones.

I'm not dead yet

We would be wrong, however, to write off the sermon just yet.

In some churches, Bible teaching is very much alive and well. Animated, down to earth, practical, humorous, inspirational speakers can hold their audience for longer than ten minutes and really connect with the issues that concern them. And theological colleges are still training preachers. Some are still full of energy for the defence of The Preacher – inextricably linked to the defence of the centrality of The Bible, or The Word.

It's not as if the spoken word is out of fashion. There's a revived interest in public speaking. President Obama's speeches have reminded people of the invigorating power of political oratory. Those with something to say still have the capacity to draw crowds. In 2009, Malcolm Gladwell sold out two nights at the Lyceum in London's West End with – wait for it – a lecture, while the Reith Lectures on the BBC continue to be highly popular as podcasts. (Indeed, the entire podcast culture is a testimony to the power of the spoken word.)

But such signs of strength may be the exception, rather than the norm. In many churches, the sermon is not something to which the congregation looks forward with high hopes. As a communication method, it faces huge challenges, not only from modern media, but also from current methods of education and teaching.

It's the old complaint

Of course, complaints about sermons are nothing new. People have been moaning about dull sermons for years – centuries even. In the fourth century, Ambrose of Milan noted, 'A tedious sermon arouses wrath.' His pupil Augustine, Bishop of Hippo, lamented the poor turn-out in his church on one feast day, had a go at the men in his congregation for being reluctant to attend church, and frequently had to tell his congregation to pay attention to him. Mind you, he did seem to be aware of the complaints about the length of his sermons. After one particularly long set of readings from Scripture, he said 'We have heard many inspired readings and I don't have the stamina to give you a sermon to equal them in length, and you couldn't take it, even if I did!'[1]

Sleeping in church has a long historical precedent. Hugh Latimer, the great Elizabethan preacher, told a story of a woman who met her neighbour and asked her where she was going. 'Marry,' she replied, 'I am going to St Thomas of Acres to the sermon. I could not sleep all this last night and I am now going hither. I never failed of a good nap there.' On 17 November, 1661, Samuel Pepys wrote in his diary that he had 'slept the best part of the sermon'.

In Elizabethan England, congregations would amuse themselves during boring sermons by spitting, telling jokes, taunting and ridiculing the preacher or simply sitting there, doing their knitting.[*]

So boring, irrelevant sermons are nothing new. Here's Anthony Trollope in *Barchester Towers*:

> *There is, perhaps, no greater hardship at present inflicted on mankind in civilised and free countries than the necessity of listening*

---

* Actually that's not a bad idea. The knitting, that is, not the spitting.

to sermons. No one but a preaching clergyman has, in these realms, the power of compelling audiences to sit silent, and be tormented. No one but a preaching clergyman can revel in platitudes, truisms, and untruisms [sic] and yet receive, as his undisputed privilege, the same respectful demeanour as though words of impassioned eloquence, or persuasive logic, fell from his lips...

While in modern times, Fred Craddock has written that 'week after week [people] return to their hard chairs before dull pulpits to hear a preacher thrash about in a limbo of words relating vaguely to some topic snatched desperately on Saturday night from the minister's own twilight zone.'[2]

Nothing changes. William Hogarth's 1736 engraving The Sleepy Congregation *delights in the detail. The hourglass has emptied, but the preacher continues. And his text? 'Come unto me all ye that Labour and are Heavy Laden and I will give you Rest.'*

The difference between Craddock, writing in the twentieth century, and Trollope, in the nineteenth, is that, today, church going is no longer a social convention. The preacher in Trollope could drone on, safe in the knowledge that everyone would still be there next week. Not so today. Today, people have a choice.

> ALWAYS celebrate and proclaim good news
> – because Jesus IS good news

Those who are there want to be there, which means the complaints are coming from people who care. Very few preaching books seem to take account of this. Most assume that those who complain about sermons have an axe to grind or simply lack the ability to listen. But the critics are not unintelligent. They are often theologically informed and passionately concerned about the proclamation of their faith. Their judgments cannot be dismissed as minority criticism. These are fans, family, friends. They deserve to be listened to.

Greetings, earthlings, we come in peace

The same is true of us. This is not an anti-preaching book. Both of us are active in teaching and preaching – and, indeed, in the teaching of preaching. We understand the difficulties and delights of being a preacher. We're not here to have a go at you, really we're not.

Preaching the gospel and teaching discipleship are part of the DNA of the Church: as much a part as prayer, giving and sharing the bread and wine. They are what the Early Church did from day one. But the issue which we want to explore in this book is whether the method of preaching and teaching most frequently used – the monologue sermon – is necessarily the best. What we're questioning is the received wisdom that the sermon is the *only* way of doing things. More, that the sermon, as typified by the twenty-minute monologue – is *God's* way of doing things – the sanctified, ordained way of teaching in the Church, unassailable and inviolable.

Too many books on preaching start from this assumption. They start from the core belief that The Sermon is the ordained will of God and his method for saving all humankind. The Sermon is sacrosanct, as sanctified a part of the service as, say, the Eucharist. The argument of this book is that is simply not true. As we hope to show, the sermon itself – certainly in the form to which we are accustomed – has not always been a part of the teaching of the church. The twenty minute monologue is not biblically ordained.

'Hold on a minute', you say, 'Jesus preached sermons, didn't he? And Peter and Paul. Not to mention all those prophets.'

Hmmm. Let's start with a bit of history.

HENRY SERMON – A LIFE WORTH FIGHTING FOR

News that Henry Sermon is fighting for his life has caused dismay in many quarters. 'This could be the end of an era,' said a hospital spokesperson. 'Well, I say "era", I mean "flipping long time". This is one seriously old dude.'

Debates are raging, though, over exactly how old Mr Sermon is. 'His birth records are either confusing or completely missing,' said the spokesperson. 'I suggested cutting one of his legs off and counting the rings, but apparently this only works with trees.'

Early years

Speaking from his newly installed media centre at the University of Badenbadenwurtemflugenstaffenberg, Professor Heinz von Beanztin told us that Mr Sermon was born in the mid-second century AD. 'His father – Mr Sermon Sr – was a rabble-rousing street preacher who worked the alleys and market squares of the Græco-Roman world,' he told us. 'His mother, Homily, however, was a former Miss Rhetoric and was largely responsible for making the family "more respectable". It may be that Henry himself still feels these tensions deep down. I blame the parents.'

Despite this, early accounts indicate that his childhood seems to have been not only happy, but vibrant and even exciting. Although he was working for the Christians – at that time an illegal organization – he seems to have had the freedom to try out different ways of teaching.

'He had a lot of different jobs in his youth,' explained the Professor. 'At one time he was a verse-by-verse biblical exegete, at another a simple storyteller. It must have been an exciting time for him, as he discovered more about the Bible and helped to form, encourage and resource a group of counter-cultural believers.'

Mr and Mrs Sermon Sr in their later years. The portrait of Henry in the background dates from his Reformation period.

It was when Christianity was adopted by the Roman Empire that Mr Sermon found his freedom curtailed. Suddenly he was working for the government. His workload – and his listeners – vastly increased. Also, for the first time he had to work in large, purpose-built churches, putting a strain on his voice that has never quite been overcome.

'Loosen up, man'

'I know from some of our sessions that, during this time and right into the Middle Ages, he felt constrained and cramped,' said his therapist, Dr Larry Pepper. 'He was obliged to adopt a fairly rigid three-point posture. That still causes him difficulty. Whenever he tries anything new these days – whenever he's inventive or playful – he feels guilty. He soon reverts to the rather stiff, formal attitudes of his former years. I used to say to him, "Henry, baby, loosen up, man." But he just couldn't.'

Things changed again for Mr Sermon in the Reformation when he was, willingly or unwillingly, thrust onto centre stage. 'People like Calvin and Luther loved him,' said Dr Pepper. 'They built the show around him. And it got even bigger in the nineteenth century when he was packing out music halls, cathedrals and lecture halls. He was a star. But I don't know if he was ever really happy with that. I mean, he loved going to new places – there was a bit of his father in him which made him keen to break new ground. There were several points in the eighteen and nineteenth centuries when he would leave the church and run into the fields, pubs or streets. But I don't think he wanted the adoration.'

Fighting for life

The latest news is that Mr Sermon is still fighting for his life.

'It's amazing,' said the hospital spokesperson, 'He's not going without a fight. Maybe part of him still wants to get out, to experiment, as he did at the beginning. **It's just been so long that perhaps he has forgotten how.'**

Part One
Medical History

The sermon isn't biblical

'Jesus came preaching' begins one multi-volume history of preaching.[3] But it's not quite as simple as that. Because, whilst there is a lot of preaching in the Bible, there is hardly anything that qualifies as a sermon, as we would understand it. Jesus might have been a preacher, but he wasn't a preacher of sermons.

Many books link the preaching of sermons to the ministry of Old Testament prophets. John Stott, for example, writes

> *First, God spoke through the prophets, interpreting to them the significance of his actions in the history of Israel and simultaneously instructing them to convey his message to his people either by speech or by writing or both.[4]*

Hughes Oliphant Old agrees, seeing in the book of Amos, for example, 'an easily recognisable sermon'.[5] But these weren't really sermons. The prophets weren't operating in any kind of liturgical or worship setting. They were street preachers, rabble-rousers, addressing their oracles to any crowd they could gather round them. Or, if their message was for the king, they headed straight to the top and issued their message from God.

And while they did convey this message 'either by speech or by writing', they also used actions. Hosea lived out God's message to Israel through the ups and downs of his married life. Ezekiel, of course, is well-known for his dramatic mimes, including cutting off and weighing his hair, and cooking pauper's bread over a fire made from animal dung. Jeremiah hid his underwear in a rock and wore a yoke round his neck to symbolise the oppression of Judah, and Isaiah stripped naked for three years![6] Try that in your church and see how the elders react.

It wasn't just the major players, either. Ahijah tore Jeroboam's new cloak into twelve pieces, returning ten to Jeroboam, to show that he would rule over ten of Israel's tribes.[7] Even false prophets got in on the act: in 1 Kings 22:11, a prophet called Chenannah made for himself 'horns of iron' and prophesied that Ahab would wipe out the Syrians. He was wrong, but it shows how popular the use of mime and costume was. Even in the New Testament we see Agabus taking his belt and symbolically 'binding' Paul.[8] And there are many more examples.

Even if we do just concentrate on the 'speech and writing' part, what the prophets didn't do is confine themselves to one form or genre. Prophetic writing includes poetry, parable, apocalyptic descriptions, and sheer, downright invective. Similarly, spoken oracles take a variety of forms, from the extended street preaching of Amos to Nathan's bedtime story to King David. And the most common prophetic form is poetry. They also used songs and even borrowed from the funeral service.[9]

So we're looking at people who frequently framed their messages in poetry, who told stories, shouted invective, sang songs and acted out mimes, and who did so outside of the religious services of their day. Sound like preachers to you? Nope, me neither.

You can't pick and choose. Yes, the prophets gave speeches and wrote stuff down, but they also performed actions and used visual aids. If you're going to cite the prophets as a mandate for the sermon, then (a) go and preach in the street and (b) take your clothes off. Or at least grow a beard.

Did Jesus preach sermons?

All right, maybe not the prophets then, but didn't Jesus preach sermons?

The gospels tell us that Jesus 'went throughout Galilee, teaching in their synagogues and proclaiming the good news of the kingdom...' (Matt. 4:23). In our church-based culture, we assume that synagogue-teaching equals preaching a sermon.

Take the most famous instance of Jesus' synagogue-preaching: the visit to his home town of Nazareth (Luke 4). It's been called the 'ground zero of preaching', forming 'a tradition of preaching that has survived with so little change that [it] might amount to instructions for a Christian service anywhere in the world on any Sunday.'[10]

But when we look at that scene closely, we can see that isn't quite the case...

In the synagogue at Nazareth

When he came to Nazareth, where he had been brought up, he went to the synagogue on the sabbath day, as was his custom. He stood up to read, and the scroll of the prophet Isaiah was given to him... (Luke 4:16-17)

The scene in the Nazareth synagogue is the earliest account of a synagogue service.[11] The synagogue, as an institution, probably arose during the Exile, although there is considerable debate between scholars about this. It was a house of prayer – open three times a day for anyone who wished to come – but not a place of worship because, unlike the Temple, it had no altar for sacrifice. It also served as a general meeting place for the community where, on two days of the week, legal cases could be settled. It was kind of a cross between church, town hall and local community centre.

Above all, it was a house of learning. 'Draw near to me, you who are uneducated, and lodge in the house of instruction,' says the *Wisdom of Ben Sirach*.[12] And many people did that. Children were educated there and the synagogue was a venue for debate and discussion for the men of the village. However it was the Sabbath which was the high point of the week. Women and children went to the synagogue as well, although they did not take an active part in the services.[13]

So, what might Jesus have found when he went into the synagogue on the Sabbath, 'as was his custom' (Luke 4:16)? The service began with prayers, led by one man, then came the reading of the Law. The scrolls containing the Law and the Prophets were usually kept in a leather case and wrapped in linen. The *hazzan* – a paid attendant who looked after the running of the synagogue – would take the scroll from its place, unwrap it and hand it to the first of seven readers. (The attendant mentioned in Luke 4:20 was probably a *hazzan*.)

It was important for accuracy that the Scriptures were *read* from the scroll – indeed it was forbidden to say more than one verse from memory. (The *hazzan* would stand by the reader and correct him if he made a mistake, or even stop him if he thought that a passage was coming which might shock people or make them laugh.)

So, seven readings would take place, with each reader allowed to comment on the text that they had read. The final reader – the reader of the 'last lesson' – always read from the prophets. He would take a small section, which he had chosen beforehand, then comment on it in Aramaic.[*] After that there would be a final prayer and a blessing, and possibly a psalm was sung.[14]

In other words, Jesus was the last of seven 'preachers' that day. His message is based on the prophets, and it was one which he probably selected beforehand.

Synagogue preaching

The usual form of preaching at the time of Jesus was that a man would simply expound the scriptures, after which there would be questions and answers.[**] Indeed, Jesus grew up in an atmosphere of learning where discussion and argument were everywhere. For example, the *haberim* – the Hebrew word means 'friends' – was a lay movement which sprang up in the villages of first century Judea, where groups of Jewish men would meet at night to discuss their faith. Jesus, throughout the gospels, demonstrates what Bailey calls 'skills in the rabbinic style of debate such as were nurtured in these fellowships.'[15] He did this from an early age. When his worried parents eventually find their boy in Jerusalem, he is 'in the Temple, sitting among the teachers, listening to them and asking them questions' (Luke 2:46-47).

Luke's account follows this pattern. Jesus chooses a text from Isaiah (Isa 61:1-2), then gives a very brief exposition, the nucleus of which lies in a single statement: 'Today this scripture has been fulfilled in your hearing' (Luke 4:21).

The text is usually translated so as to imply that the synagogue congregation were initially pleased with Jesus, and then changed their minds. 'All spoke well of him' says the NRSV (Luke 4:22). But the text literally means 'they witnessed him', perhaps meaning 'witnessed against him', as suggested by Jeremias.[16] What is clear is that the listeners were not silent. Jesus was speaking in a place of discussion, debate and – as happens here – heated exchange. This sermon was not a monologue, but

---

[*] Jesus's invitation to speak in Nazareth is echoed in Acts 13:15, where Paul and Barnabas are invited to give a 'word of exhortation' by the synagogue officials in Antioch and Pisidia.

[**] There are other forms of synagogue preaching recorded, but they all date from a time long after Jesus.

a vigorous debate. Jesus even predicts their responses, quoting a popular proverb: 'Physican, heal yourself.'

So why were they so angry? The answer lies in what Jesus does with the Scripture. When we compare the text of Isaiah 61:1-2 with the verses recorded in Luke, we can see that Jesus takes serious liberties with the original text. To be precise, Jesus:

- omits a complete line from the original (about binding up the brokenhearted)
- compresses or combines some statements about providing liberty to the captives
- adds in a reference to the blind
- introduces a phrase from an entirely different passage: 'to let the oppressed go free', from Isaiah 58:6.

Most significantly, he stops reading at the climax – when Isaiah talks about vengeance. He cuts off the end of the prophecy.

Has Jesus misquoted? Has he got muddled up? Has Luke got his reporting wrong, or re-edited and amended the text? In fact, Luke's account fits perfectly with what we know of synagogue practice. Unlike the Law, where the reader was corrected and supervised, speakers were allowed to take some liberties with the prophets. A line in the *Mishnah* – the collection of Jewish oral law – says, 'They may leave out verses in the Prophets but not in the Law. How much may they leave out? Only so much that he leaves no time for the interpreter to make a pause.'[17]

The interpreter was the person who translated the reading from Hebrew to Aramaic, since not everyone understood Hebrew. So the reader could skip verses, or select other verses, while the translator was translating the verse before! The passage in Luke, therefore, reflects the reality. It was perfectly permissible for someone to edit and truncate the Scripture readings.

So Jesus edits the text, adds in a bit from somewhere else, cuts off the crowd-pleasing ending, then sits down and says that it refers to him anyway. In the politically charged atmosphere of Galilee – an area which had suffered acutely under Roman oppression – omitting the bit about vengeance would have been provocative. But he compounds the offence in his talk by referring to two other biblical episodes – Elijah in Zarephath, and Elisha's healing of Naaman the Syrian – which imply that the people of Nazareth, the people of his home town, weren't going to get much out of their relationship with him.

No wonder the room listens to him with a mounting sense of incredulity and anger. No wonder the situation explodes into violence. No wonder he is accused of blasphemy.

This passage, then, raises a lot of issues. But we can see that, with its audience interaction and its somewhat 'flexible' view of Scripture, Jesus' teaching in the synagogue at Nazareth was nothing like our sermons today. To use this event as an example of a sermon is like using the miracle of the loaves and fishes as an example of a church picnic. It's not the same kind of event. Jesus goes in there with one aim: to stir the place up. He waltzes in, edits Scripture, winds the congregation up to violence and then disappears. Try this in your own church and you would be barred from ever preaching again. Based on this performance, Jesus would fail every preaching class going.

Jesus' teaching of the disciples

The more we investigate the teaching that goes on in the Gospels, the more it becomes clear that Jesus, really, never preached a sermon in his life. The fact is that there *are* no sermons in the New Testament, an absence acknowledged by Edwards in his monumental *A History of Preaching*: '... there are probably no sermons as such in the New Testament, no texts that had been delivered orally to an assembly for evangelization, instruction, or worship.'

'Ah,' you might be saying. 'But what about the sermon on the mount?' Well, it's certainly been cited as 'the paradigm of the sermon, indeed as the Sermon of Sermons.'[18] The problem is that it's neither a sermon, nor is it up a mount.

It's never called a 'sermon' in the New Testament, which didn't have headings of that kind. The title comes from nearly four hundred years after the event, when Augustine wrote a commentary on those chapters of Matthew and called it *De sermone Domini in monte* – Our Lord's Sermon on the mount. Before then, nobody called it a sermon. Most scholars today believe it to be a collection of Jesus' speeches and sayings, rather than a single event. And the same goes for the so-called 'sermon on the plain' in Luke. Which is some of the same material. Only on a flatter bit of land.

GREAT MOMENTS IN PREACHING
No.1 – THE SERMON ON THE MOUNT RUNS INTO PROBLEMS

Since there are no big mountains in Galilee, we should probably take the Greek word *oros* to mean 'big hill'. Jesus goes up this hill with his disciples, where, like a typical rabbi, he sits down to teach his disciples. He teaches them through statements, certainly, but also through question and answer, discussion and debate.

Rabbinic teaching of the time was largely done in what you might call seminar mode. A typical session in the rabbinical schools might run like this:

1. The rabbi would propose the discussion of a certain subject.

2. He would ask a disciple to recite, from memory, some relevant teaching from the oral tradition.

3. Other disciples might chip in with other relevant teaching.

4. The rabbi would then ask the students what was meant by these various snippets of teaching. Different students would give different interpretations and a debate would follow. The rabbi would guide the discussion by questions and remarks.

5. The rabbi would conclude the discussion, giving his preferred solution, illustrating it by a parable or Scripture verse.[19]

Jesus frequently uses the same approach. He sits down, gathers his disciples around and asks them a question. Or he is asked a question himself, either by his disciples, by interested seekers, or even by his enemies.

Jesus in debate: some questions in the gospels

- Who do people say that the Son of Man is? (Matt. 16:13)

- Who is the greatest in the kingdom of heaven? (Matt. 18:1)

- Is it lawful for a man to divorce his wife for any cause? (Matt. 19:3)

- Teacher, which commandment in the law is the greatest? (Matt. 22:36)

- What do you think of the Messiah? Whose son is he? (Matt. 22:42)

- Why do the scribes say that Elijah must come first? (Mark 4:10)

- What must I do to inherit eternal life? (Mark 10:17)

- Lord, will only a few be saved? (Luke 13:23)

- Is it lawful to cure people on the sabbath, or not? (Luke 14:3)

- When is the kingdom of God coming? (Luke 17:20)

- Rabbi, who sinned, this man or his parents, that he was born blind? John 9:2

We can see this when Jesus teaches in the Temple, where he engages in lively, sometimes violent, debate. People bring questions to him and he gives them his answers, or returns another question. This is not a sermon. As Old writes

We in our day do not associate this sort of dialogue with preaching. In fact, in our day, even teaching, with its formal lectures, is often far removed from dialogue...The daily teaching of Jesus in the Temple as it is reported in all four of the Gospels obviously allowed for questions.[20]

Walking along the streets, sitting on the steps, climbing hills and sharing a meal, Jesus taught his disciples through question and answer, dialogue, debate and argument.

Tell me a story

There were several other powerful ways in which Jesus taught people and preached the kingdom of God.

Like the prophets before him, Jesus used prophetic, miraculous acts to make his point. A good example is the cursing of the fig-tree which, in Mark's gospel, is used as a comment on the activities in the Temple. In this, Jesus is following the example of many Old Testament prophets who used disruptive, unsettling dramatic acts to make their points.

Jesus' most frequently used rhetorical tool was, of course, parables: those provocative tales which opened up and explained the kingdom of God. The Gospels record that Jesus never taught without using parables (Matt 13:34). Why? Well, the obvious reason is that stories are memorable. A parable allows you to wrap your teaching up in a way that can be easily recalled, to be explored at a later date. Parables ground the teaching in reality. We remember, of course, some of the sayings of Jesus, but we remember far more of the stories, our minds full of pictures of old men running towards lost sons, of beaten-up travellers on lonely mountain roads, of vineyards and houses, wedding feasts and fields filled with rulers, vagabonds, bridegrooms, farmers, shepherds and sheep.

Stories are interactive, involving the audience imaginatively. They encourage us to enter and explore. Parables, in particular, require listeners to search out their meaning. They are sacramental: a visible sign of an invisible reality. The bread and the wine, the shepherds and the sheep, are signs of something far greater.

This form of teaching worried the disciples, who might have liked Jesus to be a more straightforward, blood and thunder kind of guy. 'Why do you keep using these parables?' they asked. 'Why not give it to them straight?'[21] Jesus' answer, like his stories, is not straightforward. He wanted to give people a chance to find out for themselves, even if that meant that some would neither see nor hear. Every story was, and is, a risk; every parable a possibility.

Jesus the teacher, then, is not someone standing on a hill and making public pronouncements. Despite our attempt to squeeze his parables, puzzles and arguments into a box marked 'sermon', they keep bursting out. His teaching is miles away from what happens in a church most Sunday mornings. It involves discussion and argument, actions and stories. It involves open-ended questions and visible signs, invention, challenge and risk.

Did the apostles preach sermons?

All right, maybe Jesus didn't preach sermons. But what about the apostles? Didn't they get out there and give it to people straight?

They certainly did. The apostles definitely preached to people. But it all depends what you mean by 'preaching'. The New Testament uses three words for teaching/preaching:

- *kerusso* (κηρυσσω), the verb, is usually translated as 'I preach' or 'proclaim'. It's related to the Greek word meaning 'herald' (it can also mean a town crier or auctioneer – anyone who lifts up their voice and claims public attention to make an announcement). κηρυγμα *kerygma*, the noun, is the word for proclamation.

- *euanggelizomai* (ευαγγελιζομαι) is related to two words: *eu* meaning 'well' or 'good' and *angelos* meaning 'messenger' (the same word that gives us 'angel'). The emphasis of this word is 'I bring a good message' or 'I bring good news' and from this we get the word 'evangelist'.

- *didasko* (διδασκω) is usually translated as 'I teach'. Jesus is called 'teacher' (*didaskalos*) when he teaches in the synagogue. Interestingly, in the Gospels and Acts, the word is synonymous with the act of proclamation and it tends to be used in the same sense as *kerusso*, but in Paul's later letters it came to mean 'teach' in the sense of handing down a fixed body of doctrine which was to be carefully learned and 'preserved intact'.[22]

To some extent the New Testament uses the terms interchangeably. For example, when Jesus sits down to teach his disciples in the 'sermon' on the mount, the word used is *didasko*. Mark talks about Jesus going through Galilee 'proclaiming (*kerusso*) the message in their synagogues and casting out demons' but in Matthew's parallel verse he talks of Jesus 'teaching (*didasko*) in their synagogues, and proclaiming (*kerusso*) the good news of the kingdom'.[23]

However, when we arrive at Acts and the letters, the distinction is clearer: teaching (*didasko*) is what you offer to Christians, whereas preaching (*kerusso*) is what you shout out in the streets. Preaching in New Testament terms is the 'public proclamation of Christianity to the non-Christian world'.[24] *Kerusso* brings people to life: *didasko* teaches them how to live. As Old writes

When the distinction is clear, then preaching is the proclamation or announcing of God's mighty acts of redemption in Christ, while teaching is the interpreting of the Scriptures, admonition to faith and faithful living, and training in righteousness.[25]

In New Testament terms, what happens in most of our churches on Sunday mornings is teaching. Delivering sermons is *didasko* not *kerusso*: it takes place within the church context, addressed to followers of Christ who are studying the Scriptures with a view to improving their discipleship. As Dodd puts it

Much of our preaching in church at the present day would not have been recognised by the early Christians as kerygma. *It is teaching or exhortation (*paraklesis*), or it is what they called* homilia, *that is, the more or less informal discussion of various aspects of Christian life and thought, addressed to a congregation already established in the faith.*[26]

There is a distinction between the two activities, but it is a distinction based on location, content and audience. Those *in* the church received teaching; those *outside* the church needed to hear preaching.[27]

If we examine the speeches and their settings recorded in Acts, we can see that hardly any of them are 'preaching' as we would understand it.

Major public speaking in Acts

	Ref. in Acts	Event	Audience
1.	1:15-22	Peter's speech to the 120	Some 120 followers
2.	2:14-40	Peter at Pentecost	Crowds of Jewish pilgrims in the streets
3.	3:11-26	Peter at Solomon's Porch	Jews in the Temple
4.	4:5-12	Peter in the trial	Sanhedrin and Temple aristocracy
5.	5:27-32	Peter on trial (again)	Sanhedrin
6.	7:1-53	Stephen's Defence	Sanhedrin
7.	10:34-43	Peter at Cornelius' house	Cornelius, his extended household and friends
8.	13:6-12	Paul's challenge to Bar–Jesus	Proconsul's court
9.	13:14-42	Paul at Antioch of Pisidia	Synagogue on the sabbath
10.	14:14-18	Paul at Lystra	Crowds in the streets
11.	17:22-34	Paul at Athens	Crowds at the Areopagus
12.	20:7-12	Paul speaks at Troas	Christians in an apartment
13.	20:17-35	Paul at Miletus	Church leaders from Ephesus and region
14.	22:1-21	Paul speaks in Jerusalem	The mob who were trying to kill him
15.	23:1-10	Paul before the Sanhedrin	The Sanhedrin in Jerusalem
16.	24:11-21	Paul before Felix	Roman governor
17.	26:1-29	Paul before Agrippa and Festus	Political leaders in Caesarea
18.	28:17-28	Paul in Rome	Roman Jews

Of these eighteen speeches, six are actually legal defences, taking place within a trial setting (nos. 4, 5, 6, 15, 16, 17) or, indeed, in the face of angry opposition (8, 14). Another significant chunk are *kerusso,* either in the form of street evangelism (2, 3, 7, 10, 11) or apologetic/evangelistic talks with local Jews (9, 18).[*] These demonstrate missionary preaching in the apostolic age, the kind of preaching which the first disciples used when talking to non-Christians. They don't reflect what went on in an everyday teaching situation where Christians were the main audience.

This is important for two reasons:

1. As we've shown above, you can't draw a biblical precedent for preaching sermons in church from evangelistic talks given on the streets of first century Græco-Roman cities. They are not the same thing at all.

2. Some preachers like to argue for a distinction between 'preaching' and 'teaching'. The argument goes something like 'You can't apply the rules and techniques of teaching to the sermon: because that's preaching, not teaching.' In New Testament terms, they are strictly correct. There is a distinction between the two activities, but here's the thing: *the distinction is not where they think it is.* The sermon, preached in church to an audience of Christians, is not preaching in New Testament terms: it is teaching.

For this reason, Peter's speech in Acts 2 – 'the first Christian sermon' as it's sometimes called – is not a sermon as we would understand it: it's an evangelistic message preached on the streets. It's *kerusso*, not *didasko*. You can argue for preaching on the basis of Acts, if you like, but unless you're outside in the streets telling people the good news, you are not preaching as Paul, Peter and the Early Church would have understood it.

Sunday school

Ok, so, if all that *kerusso* went on in the streets, what was teaching like inside the church, then?

It's actually quite hard to say for sure.

Teaching was a central activity of this new movement, especially the use of Hebrew Scriptures to illuminate and explain the life and work of Jesus, but little of this discipleship teaching is detailed in Acts and what there is has been overshadowed by the public proclamations.

---

[*] There are other instances of such talks in synagogues or Jewish meeting places, e.g. by the river in Philippi (16.11–15) and in the synagogues at Thessalonika (17:1-4) and Beroea (17:10-12). We don't have any reported speech for these meetings, but they were clearly discussions – indeed arguments – where Paul and Silas sat with the synagogue attendees and 'argued with them from scriptures' (17:2).

We have, in fact, just three instances where we are given any real detail about the content or style of teaching within the Early Church house setting (nos 1, 12 and 13 on the chart).*

The first, Acts 1:15-26, is a piece of church governance (although Peter does use Scripture to back up his argument.)

The second, Paul's address to the church leaders at Miletus (Acts 20:17-35) is also not an ordinary example, it's a meeting of local leadership, called so that Paul can say goodbye. What we have is his farewell speech, followed by prayers and then a walk down to the quayside.

The third – Paul's talk at Troas (Acts 20:7-12) – is, in fact, the only detailed picture of a Christian meeting in the New Testament. Although we hear nothing of the content of Paul's speech, we do get a vivid picture of a Christian meeting in the early years. It takes place on the first day of the week – the first recorded instance of Christians meeting on a Sunday – and the location was an *insulae*, a Roman apartment building. Basically, these Christians were meeting in someone's third-floor flat. So, not a big meeting, and not in a residence of the social elite. The meeting extended into the night, because Paul intended to leave the next day. The heat of the lamps, combined, perhaps with the subject of the discussion, causes a young man called Eutychus literally to drop off, falling out the window to his death. The story ends happily because he is restored to life and the meeting continues.

So what was the teaching like? Several translations give the impression that Paul was preaching (that he 'spoke to the people'), but the Greek word used to describe what Paul was doing that night is *dialogizomai* which means 'discuss' or 'debate' as much as 'speak'. (You can hear an echo of the word in our term 'dialogue'). The NRSV captures what was going on more accurately, reporting that 'Paul was holding a discussion with them'. F. F. Bruce writes, 'A conversation rather than an address is indicated.'[28] This is not a sermon, it's a conversation. Although it may well be that Paul gave some kind of address, there is nothing in the text to say that Paul preached. There is no mention of proclamation, not even, in fact, of teaching.

This is important: the earliest description we have of a church 'service' does not – according to the text – contain a sermon. Yet a sermon is

---

* We have omitted the Jerusalem Council in AD 49 (Acts 15) since this was clearly a church governance meeting. There is no indication that those other than the leadership were in attendance.

constantly read back into it. Writers of commentaries and translations, perhaps out of sheer force of habit, perhaps unable to envisage a meeting of the Early Church without a sermon, put the words 'preached' and 'sermon' back in to their version.*

But look at the evidence. The only 'ordinary' church meeting in Acts contains a conversation, rather than a talk. There is, in fact, a historic link between conversations and the sermon. We have two words for the speeches produced by preachers in church: homily and sermon. In this very passage, Paul is recorded as 'conversing' with his friends at Troas (Acts 20:11). The Greek word for conversation is *homileo* (ὁμιλέω) and it is from this word we get the word 'homily'. As for the word 'sermon' it comes from the Latin *sermo*, which means... wait for it... conversation.

In other words, the teaching which happens among Christians every Sunday, has its origin in the conversations shared in smoky, lamplit rooms in Troas, Ephesus and Philippi and Jerusalem and Rome – in the secret and not-so-secret meetings of followers in apartment blocks, houses and rooms above the warehouses and shops of the ancient world. Everywhere, in Paul's day, Christians met to have conversations about Jesus. Outside on the streets, where they were able, they preached the kingdom through speeches and arguments. But in their meetings, they *talked to one another*.

This may be one of the reasons why Paul is so against the tricks of rhetoric and eloquence: because such tricks derailed the conversations. Indeed, Paul was criticised because he wasn't a great orator. Certainly his one foray into the public world of Greek oratory – his speech in Athens – met a mixed reception, and a faction within the Corinthian church clearly felt that Paul's teaching lacked quality.[29] A Greek city like Corinth had a great admiration for classical philosophers and for the virtues of classical rhetoric and eloquence. Paul seems to have been criticised because he did not adopt the special garb of the orator, nor did he use the right rhetorical

---

* Acts 20:7; NRSV and ESV have 'holding a discussion' or 'talked with them'; NIV, CEV have 'spoke to the people'; KJV, NJB and The Message have 'preached' with the NJB even saying 'preached a sermon', an addition that is nowhere in the Greek text. Similarly, in commentaries: 'the sermon was a major item in the programme' Blaiklock, E. M., *The Acts of the Apostles: An Historical Commentary* (London: The Tyndale Press, 1959), 165; '[Paul] preached and at great length' Neil, William, *Acts: Based on the Revised Standard Version* (London: Marshall, Morgan & Scott, 1981), 211; 'in addition to the supper there was a sermon...' Stott, John R. W., *The Message of Acts: To the Ends of the Earth* (Leicester: Inter-Varsity, 1991), 321. Although in the latter case he goes on to suggest that it was not purely a monologue but included 'questions and answers'.

flourishes.[30] By Paul's time, the art of classical oratory had developed into something of an artificial, showboating kind of style. Paul rejects this

> *When I came to you, brothers and sisters, I did not come proclaiming the mystery of God to you in lofty words or wisdom ... And I came to you in weakness and in fear and in much trembling. My speech and my proclamation were not with plausible words of wisdom, but with a demonstration of the Spirit and of power, so that your faith might rest not on human wisdom but on the power of God (1 Cor 2:1-5).*

As for the subjects of their discussions, well, obviously there would have been the study of the Hebrew Scriptures, but also the telling and retelling of stories, the 'handing-on' of core nuggets of Christians tradition (see 1 Cor. 11:2) and a discussion of the basic responsibilities of a Christian. At various times the communities would have been visited by one of the apostles, or actual eyewitnesses of Jesus, who would pass on what they'd seen and heard.[31]

One of the earliest Christian documents, called the *Didache* – The Teaching – is a kind of discipleship manual and gives a clue as to what was discussed. (As do 1 Peter 2:11-5:11, Ephesians 4:1-6:20 and 1 Timothy). It lists different groups of church servants: prophets, ministers, teachers, exhorters, givers, leaders, and compassionate people. It assumes the presence of a fairly large body of travelling apostles and teachers and indicates that there was a *daily* teaching ministry (4:2) with the eucharist celebrated once a week, on the Lord's day.

It also contains detailed instructions on the identification of true prophets. Prophecy was a key activity in the Early Church and Paul was particularly keen that people should seek the gift of prophecy. Whether prophets could also be teachers is uncertain, but seems likely.[32] Although some people have made attempts to link prophecy with preaching, in Paul's terms, prophecy refers to spontaneous messages from God which must be tested or evaluated (1 Cor. 12:29; 1 Thess. 5:19-21).

Would the real sermon please stand up?

Let's sum up.

1. There is no biblical precedent for the twenty minute monologue to Christians. It is not a divine ordinance.

2. There is a biblical precedent for a good discussion, although we'd recommend nobody sits on the windowsill.

3. There is certainly precedent for missionary proclamation, for speaking about the kingdom of God to those who need to enter into it. That is what the New Testament defines as preaching.

4. What happens in the church on Sunday mornings is teaching, not preaching in New Testament terms. If you want to preach like Paul and Peter, go outside and buy a megaphone.

5. None of this means that the monologue-sermon is wrong. We do lots of things in church that Christians didn't do in the apostolic period (e.g. drink coffee, hand round notice sheets, play the guitar). It's just that there is no overwhelming scriptural precedent for the sermon itself.

6. Above all, we should take notice of that late-night church meeting in Troas. When it comes to the Sunday meeting of the Early Church, the only thing we have a real precedent for is conversation – not light chit-chat, but deep conversation: discussion, dialogue – *homileo* and *sermo* – homily and sermon, in their truest, original form.

What happened next

So there we have it. A potted history of the sermon – or lack of it – in biblical times. The first actual sermons we have – in the form of a longish talk – come from around 150 AD. Since that time, the sermon has firmly established itself as the *de facto* method of Christian teaching.

The reason for this was as much practical as anything else. Once the Church started growing, there needed to be a way of teaching bigger groups of people. And when Christianity became the official religion of the Roman Empire in the early fourth century, the Church took on the trappings of the empire. It built churches in the style of imperial judgment halls, and the sermon took on the style of official, imperial pronouncements, obeying the rules of rhetoric and the style of Roman oratory. You could have a discussion with twenty people in a third floor

GREAT MOMENTS IN PREACHING
No.2 – BERNARD LAUNCHES THE CRUSADES

flat in Troas; when you have hundreds of people in a cathedral you have to give them a lecture.

From then on, the sermon has been somewhat conflicted. Its privileged position has meant it could be used and abused; for every preacher willing to challenge the social order, there have been others (many others, normally) prepared to act as the mouthpiece of the government. In the hands of preachers like John Chrysostom in Byzantine Constantinople and Martin Luther King in modern America, the sermon has been an inflammatory, anti-establishment message; in the hands of preachers like Urban II and Bernard of Clairvaux, it launched the crusades.

For 1850 years, then, the twenty-minute (or so) monologue has been part and parcel of church life. It's come to be seen as the norm, the only way of teaching in church. But, as we've demonstrated, the sermon is a church tradition, rather than a biblically-ordained practice. That means that we can change things if we wish. We are at liberty to take liberties.

And there is a need for change. Because after 1850 years, the sermon is beginning to show its age.

HENRY SERMON: 'STILL CRITICAL' SAY TOP DOCS

Doctors treating Henry Sermon, who collapsed last week, have denied that the 1850 year old is in a critical condition.

'No, we said he was *criticised*, not critical,' said one doctor. 'That is the big problem. His main complaint is that everyone complains about him.'

Rambling, immobile

We spoke to Professor Heinz von Beanztin via his 3D video-conferencing facility at the University of Badenbadenwurtemflugenstaffenberg.

'Oh, people have been complaining about Henry for many years,' he told us. 'Of course, there are things about him that we cannot change – character flaws, as it were. But a lot of the complaints are more the way he presents himself. You know, he comes across as a stiff, immobile, rambling old man, who is stuck in the past. No wonder people have trouble paying attention to him. Now, if you'll excuse me, I have an interview to do for the BBC.'

'Doing all we can'

Doctors meanwhile, say that they are doing all they can to help, but that Henry himself has to want to get better.

'It's really a question of whether he's going to listen to us,' they say. 'You can't help anyone who doesn't actually think they're ill. Also, the fact that he's hard of hearing doesn't help: if you do try to engage with him and ask questions, either he can't hear you or he goes on for hours about Martin Luther.'

'It could go either way. At the moment, we've put him in the bed between Mr 35mm Camera and Mrs Letter Writing. We'll just have to see if he can pull through.'

Delusions of grandeur

Other sources in the hospital report that Henry is prone to massive mood swings and that there are even fears for his sanity. 'Some days he suffers from delusions of grandeur,' said a source. 'He goes around shouting things like "Don't you know who I am?" and "I used to be important" to any passing member of staff. At other times he seems nervous of speaking out, scared of the world around him.'

All is not lost however. Doctors are suggesting that if he will only take his tablets he will be fine. 'I think he's got a lot of admirers, really, the old boy. And let's face it, a lot of people rely on him each week. So they should be willing to take a hand. As long as he'll let them help him.'

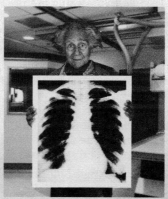

Henry Sermon undergoing X-Rays at the hospital. According to doctors the X-Rays revealed a 'significant lack of substance'.

Part Two

Complaints and Remedies

How serious is it, Doc?

You don't have to speak to many church-goers before dissatisfaction with the sermon starts to arise. In fact sometimes you don't have to talk to church-goers at all. The day after signing contracts on this book, I was at a literary festival, where, in a café, I overheard two women talking about how good and interesting the speakers had been. Then, without warning, they suddenly began to compare them with what they'd heard in church. And one of them said

> If you're only 50-50 about going [to church] then the sermon can tip you one way or the other. It can be a real turn-off. Some of them are still speaking in the same way I heard fifty years ago.

That woman's comment has been echoed, in various ways, in the many conversations we've had with people during the course of writing this book.

The sermon is ill. It's suffering from a number of serious complaints. The illness may not be terminal, but it is serious. Broadly speaking, the complaints from which the sermon suffers fall into three distinct types.

Problems with form

Complaint 1: The sermon has delusions of grandeur
Complaint 2: The sermon is eminently forgettable
Complaint 3: The sermon is old

These are endemic, built-in problems and they're the toughest, because they're part and parcel of the form itself. The twenty-minute monologue is, by its very nature, easily forgettable. By nature it is also authoritarian.

Those problems are hard to deal with in a society with a short attention span and little respect for authority.

Problems with content
Complaint 4: The sermon is short-sighted
Complaint 5: The sermon is hard of hearing
Complaint 6: The sermon is rambling and confused

These are problems with the subject of the sermon, with its rambling nature or its irrelevance. Time to get in touch with the people we're talking to. And start listening to people – get a hearing aid.

Problems with presentation
Complaint 7: The sermon lacks energy
Complaint 8: The sermon lacks mobility
Complaint 9: The sermon is short of breath

These are problems with movement, voice or mannerisms – structure, too. On the face of it these are superficial and a bit of exercise should do the trick.

So, in this part we're going to look at nine specific sermon complaints. In each case, we'll describe the complaint in detail then suggest some possible remedies. At the end of each section, we'll make three specific suggestions for use in preaching team meetings or for personal reflection.

If you find these remedies too tame, keep reading. Part 3 will look at Alternative Therapies – ways of doing without the sermon altogether.

Problems with form

Complaint 1: Delusions of grandeur

Let's admit it, those of us who preach think we're a bit special.

You can't fail to notice it when reading books about preaching. A sense of supreme self-importance pervades the pages. Many books of 'homiletics' are filled with people talking about the specialness of their job, the uniqueness of their calling.

And this has been going on since the Middle Ages. From the Grand Master of the Dominicans, Humbert de Romans, through to John Wycliffe and Erasmus, when the Reformation church gave centrality to the sermon, when 'The pulpit was higher than the altar.'[33]

One reason why people held this opinion was as a corrective: preaching had fallen into a terrible, ignorant state and they were trying to restore its reputation. But this high view of sermon-preaching seems to have gained an unstoppable momentum in succeeding centuries, even when the sermon was under no such threat.

During the golden age of Victorian preaching, James Alexander, the first professor in the new Princeton Theological Seminary, wrote: 'The pulpit will still remain the grand means of affecting the mass of men. It is God's own method and he will honour it',[34] while Charles Silvester Horne depicted the preacher as an almost godlike figure

> *The preacher, who is the messenger of God, is the real master of society; not elected by society to be its ruler, but elect of God to form its ideals and through them guide and rule its life ... This is the world's unconquerable and irresistible Hero. All its most enduring victories are his.*[35]

And there are plenty of twentieth-century writers and preachers who would agree. 'God's own method?' Really? I wonder, sometimes, whether in all the history of Christianity, any other set of people have so consistently bigged themselves up.*

In the nineteenth century, preachers were, indeed, superstars. Spurgeon preached to crowds of ten thousand in the Surrey Music Hall. The most

---

* Well, maybe if you count the Popes. But there were less of them.

popular preacher of his day, he oversaw the building of the Metropolitan Tabernacle in London. It had a capacity of six thousand, and Spurgeon filled it twice every Sunday for thirty years.

Now, however, those days are long past. And today such lofty pronouncements about preachers look, at best, an over-estimation and, at worst, smug and self-congratulatory. The pulpit no longer confers automatic authority. Just because we've got the microphone and a bigger Bible than anyone else doesn't immediately confer respect. If people are going to listen to us it will be because of our integrity, not because we pull rank.

GREAT MOMENTS IN PREACHING
No.3 – SPURGEON ORGANISES REFRESHMENTS

A challenge to authority

The problem is that our relationship with authority has changed. As Craddock writes

> *It is generally recognised that many blows struck against the pulpit come not only because of its peculiar faults but because it is a part of a traditional and entrenched institution, and all such institutions – religious, political or otherwise – are being called into question.*[36]

This process has been going on for quite some time. In 1982, John Stott wrote that 'seldom, if ever, in its long history, has the world witnessed such a self-conscious revolt against authority ... All the accepted authorities (family, school, university, state, Church, Bible, Pope, God) are being challenged.'[37]

Since then the pace of change has only increased. We no longer trust our politicians or newspapers to tell us the truth. We double-check the diagnoses from our doctors. We are the Wikipedia generation; everyone is an expert. We might look at such developments with regret and, heaven knows, Wikipedia is a long way from being infallible, but the fact is that people won't just listen to what they are told any more. They want to find out things for themselves.

Few areas show this as much as our relationship with politicians. The old-style, patrician politicians, are a thing of the past. Take this exchange in 1955 between leader of the Labour Party, Clement Attlee, and a BBC reporter

> *BBC reporter: Would you like to explain Labour's plans for the election campaign?*
>
> *Clement Attlee: No.*[38]

You wouldn't get away with that today. Today's politician has to be approachable, engaging, able to answer questions. They have to show us that they understand. They cannot stand aloof any more.

Now, in politics, as in preaching, the spoken word – the speech – is still important. As we've already mentioned, Obama's recent successes show just how great an impact a great orator can have. But the key thing about someone like President Obama is that he is not just a great orator – he is a great communicator. He has mastered a wide variety of different media.

Kathleen Hall Jamieson has analysed the speaking skills of twentieth century American presidents. It is those who know how to relate to people, how to use visual images, who succeed. Presidents like Lyndon B. Johnson and Jimmy Carter were seen as too preachy and pompous. It was the chatty, informal Reagan who knew how to work the media in the televisual age.[39] We don't want the paternalistic 'We know what's good for you' politician or preacher; we want someone with whom we feel we can have a dialogue.

The balance of power has shifted. This is the era of blogs and Twitter and Facebook, where everyone can have a say and all authority can be questioned. The relationship between consumers of information and the people or organisations giving them that information, has changed – and it would be ridiculous for us to think the Church is somehow immune to this.

Does this mean the death of the sermon? No. But it definitely means the death of the self-important preacher. And shouting 'Do you know who I am?' won't work. As Churchill observed, 'I know of no case where a man added to his dignity by standing on it.'

In dealing with an illness, the first thing the patient needs to do is admit there is a problem. The longer we persist with the idea that preaching is perfect, that it is 'God's own method,' the less likely we are to do something about it; the more we insist on our authority, the more likely it is that our listeners will assert theirs. Often, simply by heading for the exits.

In denial

All of this means that, methodologically the sermon is under fire. It's looking over its shoulder at a load of fresh, new, up-and-coming means of communication and, although it would never admit this to anyone, it's slightly depressed.

It's been mugged by more powerful means of communication and technology; it's often the subject of mockery and derision. People who used to listen to it with awe are now arguing back or – worse – ignoring it entirely. Its defenders defend it with a passion, but often sound a note of false confidence. Their bravado is a little too strong, their voices a little too loud.

It's strange when reading books on preaching to see how often the fundamental questions and concerns are simply brushed away as if they don't matter. There is barely a mention of any alternatives, virtually no acknowledgement that there might actually be a different way of doing things. Instead, alternatives to the 'Service of the Word' are dealt with in a few glib paragraphs, caricatured and misrepresented so that they can easily be brushed aside.

Paradoxically, this show of strength betrays a lack of confidence. Let's pretend that the problems don't actually exist; better still, let's accuse anyone who raises objections of being fundamentally unsound (or possibly heretical). Then we don't have to deal with any of the real issues.

The sermon doesn't have to be depressed. It doesn't have to tone down its message. But it does have to explore the possibility that it might need to change. Just a bit.

Otherwise, all this repression can't be good for it. You know what happens if you refuse to admit to any problems, if you bottle it all up.

We could be heading for a breakdown.

Remedies for delusions of grandeur

Get a sense of perspective

First, it would be good if all of us who preach admitted that the sermon is not the be all and end all. The sermon is, undoubtedly, an important part of Church life, but it is just one part. Too many churches engage in a kind of sermonolatry: they have turned the sermon into a false god. It's very easy to create a god: you just put something on a pedestal and then expect miracles from it. By putting both preachers and the sermon on a pedestal, we have, in the end, done them a disservice. We've raised our expectations far too high. Time to come down to earth.

- Every sermon has the chance to change someone's life. But then again, people hear a lot of sermons.
- Every sermon has the chance to change someone's life. But that doesn't mean that there won't be another one along next week.

- Every sermon has the chance to change someone's life. But then again, so does every conversation, so does every prayer.

We're not being flippant here, or defeatist, or complacent. We must be realistic about what the sermon can and can't achieve. The point is that sermons are only part of the mix, only one of many ways in which the Holy Spirit draws people towards God. The sermon is a really important part of the ministry of the Church: but then no more than any other. This is the kind of truth that many pay lip-service to, but few of us really believe. People talk about the 'body' and the way in which 'we all play a part', while all the time a secret hierarchy is forming in our minds, with the big names, the platform party, the ones running the big churches, the ones – heaven forbid – with their names on the spine of the books, the people who get into the pulpit, all jostling for position. We may talk about the 'priesthood of all believers' but, to paraphrase Orwell, some priests are more equal than others.

What we think is most important on earth, may not be the most important thing in the eyes of heaven. The magnificent message preached from the pulpit that Sunday morning may not have the angels partying as much as the conversation that occurs over coffee. This is not to say that you scrap one and concentrate on the other. The sermon, too, is a service of faithfulness – and, that's what makes it so special. But it is part of the mix. It's not the be all and end all.

Why do we need to acknowledge this? Because love is blind. Those of us who love preaching and are passionate about the sermon, and who have sacrificed huge amounts of time and effort to the task, find it difficult to admit that there is any need for change or improvement. The same attitude doesn't work in the rest of life. If a manufacturer thinks their product is perfect, they're never going to carry on developing it. And the world is full of discarded products which the manufacturers thought could never get any better. It's full of people who were so in love with their product (or their event, their programme, their idea) that they were completely taken by surprise when people stopped wanting it.

Continue to learn

The 'grand' delusion about sermons is that we think we've made it when we step onto the platform. Because we prefer to do the speaking rather than the listening, we can be complacent and, sometimes, downright unteachable. 'We've got heaps of experience – we don't need any more training, thank you.'

But there's a big difference between the approach of a professional and an amateur: the professional never stops learning. You notice this about people who really are at the top of their game: they don't stop seeking improvement. Piano *virtuosi* still practise their scales, great film directors still go to the movies. The England rugby player, Johnny Wilkinson, still spends two hours practising his goal kicking before every test match – this after ten years as an international and seventy caps. One corrective to delusions of grandeur is to recognize, however well it went, we could always have been done it better.

We should have the humility to learn from anyone who can help us improve: ordained or lay, in Christian ministries or in other spheres of work. There are a lot of great teachers and speakers out there from whom we can take notes. Look at great presenters and speakers at work.[*] We can learn from other professions. We rarely learn from school teachers, for example, who are an obvious source of expertise. Keep reading up on the subject.

We have to be able to justify our place on the preaching team.

Join the team
Talking of preaching teams...

Chances are, if you preach regularly in your local church, that you are part of what's called a preaching team.

'Being part of a preaching team is like being in a bowling team,' one local preacher told us. 'Each bowler has to complement, or correct, what the other bowler has put down earlier, and of course this contribution will affect the next bowler negatively or positively.' But is this what happens in practice? 'On the whole, preachers are very individualistic in approach,' observes a Church of England vicar. 'Of course, if there is a theme, then we follow one another as we can, trying to listen to or read the sermon from the week before. In reality, we stand alone and speak what we feel God is saying to us for this people at this time.'

So, can a team meeting help?

---

[*] There are links on the website.

My pastor ... identified a gift for public speaking in me; I was in leadership so spoke at members' meetings on admin matters but had also led worship times. He also knew that I routinely delivered presentations in my secular job.

The church I attended had a young adult discipleship course. With the help of leaders or mentors we were all encouraged to 'have a go' at preaching on 'Youth Sundays' or other occasions. Being able to communicate your faith through testimony or explain the truth of Scripture was seen to be very important for young Christians. Members of the congregation – especially older Christians – were very gracious, supportive and encouraging. Sincerity, integrity and enthusiasm, mixed with a desire for others to understand and grow in their own faith were valued as hallmarks of a potential preacher.

Tea Meeting or Team Eating?

In one local church, the preachers meet once every couple of months, so we asked them how well they thought they worked as a team. Was it co-operative or competitive? A real source of help? Or just a place for tea and sympathy? The reactions varied. One said 'We have a great group of people willing to give of themselves. There is great talent and enthusiasm and variety. It is an amazing place to be and come away with thanksgiving that I am not alone.' On the other hand, 'We meet too infrequently to work as a team, but as a group that meets and offers encouragement, then, yes, we work well.'

This was enthusiastically endorsed by someone newer to preaching. 'I feel I could go to several of the preaching team for ideas or thoughts if I was struggling to put a sermon together. Also, people in the group have been quick to say they are praying for me when I'm doing a sermon, and very forthcoming with encouraging feedback afterwards, which I've really appreciated.'

The team meeting can be useful for the minister, too. 'The team is able to gauge where the different congregations are coming from – and offer ideas as to what would be good to study or develop further. What one group may need – children, youth, older members, families – is different to another. The preaching group is able to share insights as to how to make the service work for everyone.' It can also build confidence. 'I sense a fear to go beyond what is comfortable. The preaching team offers encouragement to try new methods, i.e. using videos, music, drama.' There was a feeling, however, that the team could do still more. 'I feel that the preaching team should be a place to hold each other to account, offer constructive criticism – but I rarely see this happen ... I sense a level of fear and vulnerability.'

Of course, it's not always easy managing such a mixture of people: voluntary and paid, ordained and lay, with a variety of backgrounds, training and churchmanship. It can be a delicate matter encouraging everyone to share and develop but everyone can play their part. As with any team, you only get out what you put in – and being ready to learn is the primary condition for being a good teacher. 'I'm increasingly convinced,' writes one of the team, 'that to make a spiritual impact on anyone, it is the preparation of the messenger, rather than the message, that God will ultimately use.'

Take every opportunity

> *Little children were being brought to him in order that he might lay his hands on them and pray. The disciples spoke sternly to those who brought them, and Jesus said, 'You've got a point, actually. I'm a preacher, I shouldn't be doing this.' So they sent for Mary Magdalene. And lo! She did do some craft with them.*

Preaching doesn't have to be in a pulpit. If you are serious about improving as a speaker, take a range of opportunities. Speak to teenagers, to grandparents, to mums, and toddlers. Learn how to communicate to a wide variety of people.

Too many people are reluctant to take what they see as a 'step-down' and speak to smaller or younger groups; these things can get left to the curate or youthworker. But all of it can nourish our teaching skills. We will communicate better with adults if we have learnt how to communicate with children. Children and young people are not good at feigning politeness, so if they're bored, we'll know it straight away. From them we can learn the need for strong structure, visuals, energy and immediate impact.

How many senior pastors, canons, vicars or similar ever go and 'preach' to the children? Not many.[*] We think it should be mandatory.

Allow the questions

> *Bring in a story, maybe against yourself, to engage the congregation.*

Children won't listen forever. At some point, they'll want to respond. And adults do, too. This could take place during the sermon, with a question and answer time, or it might be at a separate event. It might simply be an openness to respond to criticism and questions via email, after the service or over a coffee.

Too many sermons are presented as closed books: take it or leave it messages which leave the listener feeling frustrated.

Sermons and homilies began as a conversation – and conversations take place between equals.

---

[*] That is what we have women for.

For preaching team meetings or personal reflection

1. Manage expectations

   'We must be realistic about what the sermon can and can't achieve.' Consider what you believe can happen during a sermon and be upfront about this.

   - What do I believe the sermon can and can't do?
   - What expectations do my listeners have?
   - What do I believe to be true about the way people hear from God?
   - What helps people learn to be followers of Jesus?
   - What makes people change their behaviour?
   - How much do I have to do? How much can I leave to God?

   You can think this through further by using David J. Schlafer's book *Your Way with God's Word*. Although it concentrates on style, as a workbook with space for written reflection, it gives the reader space to unpack thoughts about what preaching and teaching can do.

2. Suggest people who've never preached before and give them appropriate support to do it.

3. Offer to help and plan a session in your children's work.

Problems with form

Complaint 2: Eminently forgettable

> *Research into the effectiveness of sermons has uncovered worrying evidence that all preachers need to take seriously. North American and European studies have produced similar results: somewhere between 65% and 90% of those interviewed directly after the meeting ended could not say what the main point of the sermon was or what issue it was addressing.*[40]

Most sermons are instantly forgettable. This is not necessarily the fault of the preacher – it's the very nature of the format itself. To speak for ten minutes to an audience and keep their attention is a rare skill; to manage it for twenty minutes or even more, is much, much harder. (And to speak for anything over that and retain your audience's rapt attention you have to be either (a) very good indeed or (b) the dictator of a small communist country.) But take another look at those figures at the top: they mean that, in a congregation of a hundred, up to ninety of those listening could have forgotten the sermon by the time they hit the church door.

Should sermons be that memorable, however? Are we just pandering to modern sensationalism? In the course of discussing this book, several people have suggested that sermons are not about making a 'big splash'; they're about everyday nutrition. Here's how I found the analogy expressed on a website forum. The person posting it claimed to have taken it from an exchange of letters on 'Why go to church' in a local newspaper

> *I've been married for thirty years now. In that time my wife has cooked some 32,000 meals. But for the life of me, I cannot recall the entire menu for a single one of those meals. But I do know this: They all nourished me and gave me the strength I needed to do my work. If my wife had not given me these meals, I would be physically dead today. Likewise, if I had not gone to church for nourishment, I would be spiritually dead today!*

Hmmm. Personally I feel sorry for his wife. Imagine that – 32,000 meals, and the ungrateful man can't remember a single one of them. He was probably feeling really happy with this letter, right up to the moment the wife poured a bowl of chilli con carne on his head. He certainly remembered that meal. If I'd put a meal on the table every night for 25 years and *not one* of them was memorable I might think it time to invest in a new cookbook, or a takeaway. Or possibly a divorce.

Undoubtedly the sermons we hear do shape us; we absorb teaching and wisdom without it all being about memorable soundbites and impressive oration. But there has to be *some* of that, surely? There has to be, among those 32,000 meals, one or two memorable moments!

Same old, same old...

> Don't give the sermon in triplicate – I heard what you said the first time.

One of the reasons that the sermon is so forgettable is that it's always the same. Every week, all over the world, here's the standard package:

- Start with a joke.
- Repeat the narrative of the Scripture readings, just in case no-one was listening the first time.
- Say what we have to say, preferably in three points, all beginning with the same letter.
- Conclude, with a poem if we can find one. Or an inspiring anecdote.
- Add a closing prayer, giving time for the congregation to regain their senses.

The three-point sermon goes back to medieval times. And it's still being taught today. It's survived because it is a strong, robust, simple structure. And I'd rather have a three-point sermon than a pointless one. But it means that week in, week out we hear the same basic model.

Same language

Then there is the repetitive language. This might take the form of religious clichés, which, although undoubtedly true, fail to have their full impact if repeated often enough.

- 'God is love'
- 'Jesus loves you'
- 'We need more of the Holy Spirit'
- 'God loves a cheerful giver'
- 'Young people are the church of today, not the church of tomorrow'
- 'Fight the good fight/run the race/wrestle the waterbuffalo'
- Anything to do with the armour of God.

It's not that these aren't true – they are deep and wonderful truths – but even the greatest truths can become devalued through glib repetition.

Another form of repetition is the generalised side-swipes at the world around us:

- 'We live in an age of instant gratification'
- 'When I point the finger at you, I'm pointing four back at myself'
- 'The trouble with society today...'

Quoting from your favourite Christian author: is it really necessary, week after week?!

Not another sermon on Romans...

Preaching often covers the same themes, over and over and over again. We might have attended church for thirty years, but still never got beyond the Lord's prayer and the ten commandments.

Or perhaps every sermon is an evangelistic sermon, with a full-on call for converts. This is a wonderful thing in a church full of non-Christians, but not so effective when the congregation have made their commitment and are wondering what to do next.

Or every sermon might be about the dangers of same-sex marriage/ the lack of Christian concern for the poor/the dark night of the soul/ the Lord's apparent abandonment of Sheffield United – it just depends what the pastor is into.

> *Beware using sermons to work out your own emotional issues or promotion of pet topics.*

Most sermons also focus on a limited range of biblical material. In most churches there is a Bible within the Bible: there is the big book, with all its 66 books, and within that the small number of texts that actually get preached on. If you don't believe me, when was the last time you heard a sermon on Lamentations? Or Habbakuk?

Remedies for forgetfulness

Learn about learning

We've learnt a lot in recent years about what helps people remember and there has been a lot of interest in transferring this to the sphere of education. Kathy Sierra, for example, has produced an excellent Crash Course in Learning Theory.[41] It talks about what makes the brain work best. Some of the things listed include:

- using all the senses
- saying the same thing again – but differently
- using visuals, variety and surprise
- using stories
- building curiosity
- making the learner feel relaxed and confident.

'Don't underestimate feelings,' she says – nor the power of failure or fun. One way, apparently, to increase attention and memory is to use the brain's reaction to faces. 'The ability to accurately recognize faces and read facial expressions is a key element of survival for the brain.'

Another bit of advice is to use 'chunking' (grouping things into a memorable pattern) to help the memories get processed in the file marked 'long-term'.[*]

Here are some simple ways to make your sermon more memorable.

---

[*] We should also note that there are a lot of neuromyths out there. There's been a bit of a backlash in the noughties against a lot of the received wisdom. Sometimes in their excitement over learning styles and right brain/left brain divisions people have forgot to ask for any actual evidence. We still clearly need authoritative substantiation for claims rather than relying on personal hunches. On the other hand, these approaches can't do any harm. There's no harm in being reminded about good practice!

Make us laugh

One of the simplest ways to keep people's attention is to make them laugh. People who joke from the pulpit have always proved controversial – especially to those who have no sense of humour. Spurgeon defended humour in the pulpit saying he thought it 'less a crime to cause a momentary laughter than a half-hour's profound slumber.'*

> Make it humorous and informal – but challenge us deeply in our lives and relationship with God as you expound and apply Scripture.

Using humour in sermons is an easy win for preachers. Even the feeblest joke is almost bound to get a laugh, just because listeners are so grateful. And good jokes will have them rolling in the aisles. Not to mention up the nave and into the chancel.

However, jokes can be a double-edged sword. Too much use of humour runs the risk of detracting from and disrupting the talk, rather than enhancing it. It's far better if it can be organically connected to the theme or point you are trying to make. (People are more forgiving with jokes so if one or two of them have only a tenuous link they'll be OK – just make sure they're actually funny.)

Some people don't use humour because they don't think they are naturally funny. But there are other places to find good, humorous illustrations for your talks. You can collect amusing stories from the newspapers, or jokes which you have heard on TV or radio. Books of funny sermon stories vary hugely in quality – but stories that are written well, with economy and rhythm, will read well. Just make it clear and punchy. And don't go on too long. (But, then, that's a good rule for sermons, full stop.)

Try not to force jokes or anecdotes in. They work best when they appear as a seamless part of the sermon – when they fit perfectly with the message. Too often as preachers, we've got hold of a great story or funny

---

* He also said, 'If some men were sentenced to hear their own sermons, it would be a righteous judgment upon them; but they would soon cry out with Cain, "My punishment is greater than I can bear."'

joke and we're desperate to use it – so desperate that we will make the most obscure links to the subject matter.

> Make us laugh. Make things fun and memorable.

So... you don't have to be the world's greatest stand-up, but comedians can teach you a lot. Watch how they time their statements, use the stage, and bring their audience together as one.

It's the best kind of research – sitting in front of the television, and having a laugh – what's not to like?

GREAT MOMENTS IN PREACHING
No.4 – IN GENEVA, CALVIN TELLS A JOKE

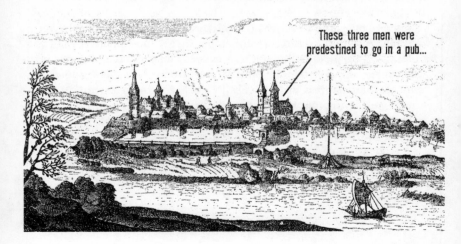

These three men were predestined to go in a pub...

Exercise your imagination

You don't just need to exercise your memory and muscles in a sermon. You need to exercise your imagination as well. Anna Carter Florence picks up this thought in her essay entitled 'The Preaching Imagination': 'Preachers who are imaginatively in shape,' she claims, 'will find it easier to make their way into the text, and easier to get out of the way during the sermon...'[42] What does that mean? It means that you help the listener use their imagination and so find their way through to independent thought, discovery and response to God.

Imagination needs to be exercised. We preachers need to develop the habit of using it, living by it, seeing through it, every day. We need to help our listeners to imagine a scene, or their response to an event. And, of course, one of the best ways to do this is to...

Tell a story

Stories draw the listener in and force them to use their imagination. They make the abstract real. That's the power of story. In which case, why not tell a story and do nothing else?

A good preacher is not only a Bible student and a prayer watchman, but also an imaginative writer. In recent years, people have been very excited to discover the first person narrator approach to the sermon. Examples can be found in various collections of sermons.[43]

There are plenty of other ways of looking at the lives of biblical characters. One is to look at the four seasons of a person's life. Begin your sermon in the 'summer' of their life, when things are going well, then go on to the 'autumn', the difficulties, through to 'winter' when things get unbearable, and on to 'spring', when hope returns. The message is that, through the goodness of God and his resurrection power, the second 'summer' can be better than the first.

Try teaching things in different learning styles.

Use props

Props is a bit of a stagey term simply meaning objects that act as a visual aid. People tend to think that visual aids are for children, but there's no reason why looking at an object should be considered childish. All God's creation is not only fascinating in its material construction, but is latent with meaning, and the use of an object to create metaphor is key to teaching. I once read a teacher's autobiography where he listed the top twenty essential attributes for a teacher. And right at the top was the ability to use metaphor. So thinking about which prop is most key to your talk is a way to discover whether you've alighted on a helpful metaphor.

You don't have to go mad – you don't have to have a Mary Poppins bag that pours forth endless props onto a table.* We're talking about disciplining yourself to think about what the most helpful image is for people. Even (or especially) if you are talking about a complex or abstract subject, it's useful to have something which grounds it. I once saw someone explain the Trinity using a packet of Angel Delight.** And a preacher who talked about honey (taste and see that the Lord is good, etc.) at a baptism service gave the jar of honey to the parents of the child as a symbol and a reminder of the occasion.

Objects can serve a more mundane purpose as well. If you've put down your notes and don't know what to do with your hands, then holding an object to illustrate the focus of your talk is helpful. It puts the focus onto the content of what you're saying, rather than on yourself.

You don't necessarily need to use the object in its most obvious functional way. A common drama exercise is to get students using an object in different ways, eg. a scarf as a hat, a book, an ice cream. The only limit to this approach is your imagination!

Props make people curious – and that's really important in setting the scene for what you are going to say in a sermon. What if you were to get a letter out of an envelope and start silently reading it? People would be so keen to know what it says! You don't need to overact your response to the letter, just genuinely read it and people will then 'read' you and your reaction. This could provide a lead in to a reading and preaching from one the New Testament letters. Alternatively you could sit down and start writing out a part of one of the letters (as if you are Paul or Peter or John or

---

* Although if you could pull a ladder out of it, that would be great.

** No I'm not going to tell you how they did it. Work it out for yourself.

an amanuensis). This is useful if you are trying to help people understand the writer and his situation or relationship to the recipients.

The best thing about using props is that they help people make the link between theology (their knowledge of God) and their everyday lives. From washing hands, to using teatowels, to eating bread or drinking wine, these images are rich in meaning – and allow your listeners to add meaning by connecting the content of your message with their lives on a Monday morning or a Thursday afternoon. Dave Meier found that

> ... *people who used imagery to learn technical and scientific information did on average 12% better on immediate recall than those who did not use imagery, and 26% better on long-term retention. And this statistic held for everyone regardless of age, ethnicity, gender, or preferred learning style.*[44]

Do something different

Stuck in a rut? Then be deliberately different. Take a book of the Bible you've never preached on for your next series. Tackle some of those horrible passages in Joshua or Judges that no-one likes to go near. Turn your three point sermon into a two pointer. Or a one pointer. Or a five pointer. Do it in the way that you would never normally do it.

Or you could drop the sermon altogether. (But we'll have more to say about that in the Alternative Therapies section.) Whatever you do, don't do the same thing that you did last week.

For preaching team meetings or personal reflection

1. Find your least well-known part of the Bible and discuss how different well-known speakers/comedians/writers would treat it.

2. Take a Bible story and either retell it in the first person, or using the 'four seasons' approach.

3. Find the metaphor. For each sermon coming up, suggest a prop or image which might work well as a way in. (If you want to practise, take a Christian topic such as redemption, the Kingdom of God, heaven and hell, etc. and come up with a prop to explain it.)

Problems with form

Complaint 3: Old age

Let's face it, there comes a point in everyone's life when they need a Stannah stairlift. Or an electric wheelchair. Or glasses. Or anything which makes life easier.

The sermon is old technology. Of course, there's nothing inherently wrong with old technology. Spades are old technology, as are paper and pens. Yet people still need spades to dig the garden, they still write with pens on paper. The sermon has a wisdom borne of ages. It has a wealth of material to draw on. It has gravity. But gravity can tie you down.

And like most very old things (geological formations, giant tortoises, Bruce Forsyth) its reactions aren't what they used to be. Which is a bit of a problem, because all around it, the world is changing.

In the past few years, virtually everything about churches has changed. People sit in chairs or pews, which they never did in the past; the music will almost certainly have changed, with a band or electronic keyboard; and you'll probably sing pop songs, more than hymns. The liturgy has changed (albeit with a lot of effort and in the face of intense resistance) and the Bible translation is more modern. Everything has changed, but the sermon has retained its form.

The format for the sermon is usually the lecture or speech. For centuries, millennia even, the lecture/speech was the dominant form of mass communication. The lecture model was found everywhere – not just in teaching, but in religion and in politics as well. Politicians would stand on a platform and make a speech and that was how they were judged. There was no other way of judging them.

The lecture as a form of mass-communication is no longer the only way of passing on information. It has been joined by many other methods. Even within lectures themselves a range of other tools are now available, including PowerPoint, AV resources and a myriad of websites. Now we are swamped with communication methods – overwhelmed even. Think of it: TV, radio, YouTube clips, email, direct mail, newspaper articles and interviews, Twitter, Facebook, SMS messaging... the list goes on.

So the lecture or presentation is no longer merely a spoken monologue, it's a rich blend of different kinds of media. But does church teaching acknowledge the presence of these new technologies? Rarely. The only technological change that seems to have had an impact on the sermon is the printing press, and that was four hundred years ago.[45]

The lesson from the Media

Communication has become dynamic, fluid and very democratic. It's a two-way street. People no longer expect to just sit and listen. Their expectations are different. Today we expect the sermon to be:

- short and snappy – like YouTube
- entertaining and humorous, presented with the skill of celebrity TV presenters
- informative and wide-ranging, like a website
- down-to-earth and practical, like self-help programmes on TV or community learning
- participatory, like a phone-in or a skills workshop
- memorable, like an advert

We expect activity not passivity; involvement not just instruction; interactivity not inactivity.

The lesson from teachers

Teaching today is about participation and discovery, it's about finding out rather than being told.

In our workplaces, in our schools, colleges and universities, teaching and training is interactive. It is expected that it will be hands-on, that there will be time for questions. PowerPoint – even bad PowerPoint – is almost obligatory. The lecturer – if they are any good – will include visuals. You're expected to take notes and ask questions. And you are expected to carry on with your learning beyond the lecture. The lecture is just the start: you will have to attend seminars and workshops and experiments.

Or take something a little less academic – a work training course, for example. No training course these days would let all the trainees sit in a room for twenty minutes, listening to a speech, to then go back to the shop floor. There will be workshops and exercises, role-play and videos and lots and lots of assessment.

Now contrast that with what happens on a Sunday morning. There is a huge gulf between the way we learn in church and the way we learn elsewhere. In church you are expected to sit, listen and absorb, like a sponge. (Unless you are below the age of about eighteen, where you get to have a discussion, or do exciting stuff with paint and plasticine. Youth is *so* wasted on the young.)

> *Be interactive, involve the congregation.*

Remedies for old age

Use new technology

> *Be more creative – use, and don't be frightened of, new technology and ideas.*

If the sermon needs a little more colour in its cheeks, a little more sense of direction, then it can use some technology – whether low or hi-tech.

People often speak quite disparagingly about the use of equipment in a sermon, as if it's too flashy and a sign that there is no substance to the theology, a desperate attempt to hold the attention and interest of those listening.

Whilst people who react like this may be doing so because they've had their fill of object lessons and DVD clips, we don't have to throw the baby out with the bathwater. We just need to be more sparing and less fussy in the use of them. The equipment needs to *support* the talking point, not *become* the talking point.

The Power of Powerpoint

In April 2007 Powerpoint hit the headlines. 'No point to Powerpoint' roared *The Telegraph* in the UK. 'Research points the finger at Powerpoint', yelled *The Sydney Morning Herald*. 'Free Gavin and Stacey CD' screamed *The Sun*, ignoring the story altogether.

The research came from Professor John Sweller of the University of South Wales, who said

> *The use of the PowerPoint presentation has been a disaster ... It is effective to speak to a diagram, because it presents information in a different form. But it is not effective to speak the same words that are written, because it is putting too much load on the mind and decreases your ability to understand what is being presented.*

The story led to much comment on the PreachingTodayblog about the benefits and dangers of PowerPoint and other such programmes. Some reckoned it was a 'no-brainer', others admitted they felt divided on the use of slides, perhaps because it seemed to take too long to produce slides of good quality.

All agreed that a few well chosen images were helpful – perhaps a dozen at most.

> Use audio visual presentations – not just words – with interactive methods.

It's not about PowerPoint as such, it's about how you use it. One of the masters of this kind of display – unsurprisingly – is Steve Jobs, CEO of Apple, whose presentations always make a splash.[*] The main secret is simplicity – and keeping text to a minimum. The average PowerPoint slide, apparently, has forty words on it, but in a Jobs presentation you might only find seven words in ten slides. Carmine Gallo, author of a book on Jobs' presentation style, advises people to avoid bullet points – they're the least effective way to learn. Instead, Gallo advises people to eliminate the clutter: images speak volumes.

---

[*] Nick has asked me to point out, being a Mac obsessive, that Jobs uses Keynote, not PowerPoint. Happy now?

In his promotional video for the book, Gallo said

> *As long as you have a product or service, or a company or a cause that is improving somebody's life, I think you have a story to tell. Now you can either make that story really boring or really interesting, but I think, more often than not, there are compelling stories. You just have to draw out the stories – and that's what Steve Jobs does best.*[46]

Other tips from Jobs' performances include:
- Give a demo – show and tell with real props
- Create a water cooler moment – the point everyone remembers and talks about afterwards – perhaps in church you should aim for a coffee moment! (Jobs often introduces these by pretending that the presentation has ended and then adding 'Oh, and just one thing more...')
- Break it up every ten minutes with something different. Neuroscientists say that people weary of concentrating beyond that time
- Share the stage – bring in other expert voices[*]

Putting the words on a screen and then reading the exact same words is (Power)pointless. Instead, we can explore the technology to much greater effect, mixing pictures, DVD clips, sound files, maps, anything which adds a useful image or background to the sermon.

Lend me your ears
If you have a PA in your church you can play more through it than just your own voice! (Even if you don't have a PA, you can use a portable CD player). So consider using different voices and sounds. You can play excerpts from speeches or music, or different sounds. When you are talking about the Psalms, for instance, why not see if you can get a recording of a *shofar* or other Jewish instruments? For the Bible reading, you could have a snatch of the original Greek (or the even more original Aramaic).

---

[*] Go to the 43rd Point website for links which show Steve Jobs – and other great communicators – in action.

Podcast your pearls

Technology not only helps people get more out of the sermon, it can help the sermon get out more. More and more people are podcasting recordings of their sermons. For a diverse, content-hungry audience, technology like this can help your sermon escape the clutches of church.

If your church hasn't yet caught on to this idea and you're a podophobe like me, the easiest way is to find someone with technical know-how among your family or friends. With their help, listening to your first podcast is only a few clicks away – and will probably only take about five minutes to set up initially. After that, downloading individual sermons will depend on your internet connection speed.

If you, or they, need guidance on how to get going, there are many sites on the internet that give advice on how to download podcasts, but you will need to find the instructions appropriate to the equipment you own. For instance, if you own a Mac computer, you will already have iTunes installed. If you have a PC, you will need to check. If you don't want to subscribe to iTunes, you may need some other 'media aggregator' software such as Juice.[*]

> ### For preaching team meetings or personal reflection
>
> 1. Get an expert in! Arrange some training on the use of PowerPoint or modern audio visual equipment.
> 2. Identify the teachers in your church and invite them to your meeting – then pick their brains for good ideas.
> 3. Pick a Bible passage and suggest appropriate music or sound effects.

---

[*] For more information on podcasting, go to the 43rd Point website: www.43rdpoint.org

Problems with the content

Complaint 4: The sermon is short-sighted

In many churches, every Sunday, a huge number of invisible people sit in the pews. It's not that they can't be seen, of course, it's just that they are rarely looked at and hardly noticed. Their presence, or absence make hardly any difference to the sermon, because the preacher doesn't really see them at all.

Do you know who is in your audience? How much do you know about them? Pastors of megachurches may have their work cut out knowing who's in the auditorium, but with small to medium-size congregations, there's no excuse for not knowing names. After all, school teachers get their heads round a new lot every September. A good teacher knows each of their students, what they're capable of, and what engages their interest. As preachers, do we really know our congregation? Do we see things through their eyes?

When our eyesight is poor, we end up preaching stuff which fascinates us but which leaves the congregation cold.

What shall we tell them this term?

Here's how it goes. The preaching team or the church leadership sit down and think, 'What are we going to preach on?' Maybe it's suggested by something someone's read, something which stirs them and, one hopes, which they feel God wants the congregation to hear.

But how often do we actually ask the congregation what they want to learn about, or what they need to know? Far too often, we work from the top down. We choose the sermon series, we decide the method of delivery, we pay little attention to the real needs of the congregation. The result is that we end up answering questions they haven't asked in a language they can't understand. And then we wonder why they don't come back.

I once went to speak at a new church plant on an estate. They asked me to speak on the subject of happiness. When I asked how they'd come to pick that subject, the church leader replied, 'Well, we went round the estate asking people what they wanted to hear about.' (They also, incidentally, asked when people wanted to meet and found that the best time for their church was Thursday night.)

> *Don't make assumptions on the level of knowledge of your audience.*

A good teacher knows their pupils and what they need to learn next.

We're not saying that everything you try to communicate has to be what your audience wants to hear or see – that's the way of populist politicians or the tabloid newspapers. Sometimes it may be necessary to give a message which is potentially unpalatable or challenging. But you will only know what people need to hear if you understand who they are.

I don't get out much these days...

On the whole, the sermon stays safely within the confines of the church topics, theology and biblical studies – with nary a glance at global issues, political matters or the media, all things which hugely affect our day-to-day lives.

> *Make it interesting and relevant to today, crossing the bridge from the Bible to modern day application.*

The subject of sermons is increasingly irrelevant, dealing with issues which often don't seem that important to the average person in the pew. Karl Rahner, the Jesuit theologian, wrote

> *Many leave the church because the language flowing from the pulpit has no meaning for them; it has no connection with their own life and simply bypasses many threatening and unavoidable issues...*[47]

But calls for the sermon to bear more relevance to the outside world are often met with withering contempt.

For example, David Jackman's number one point in his chapter 'From Text to Sermon' runs: 'Get rid of the idea that we have to make the text relevant.'[48] Another writer grumbles that 'The pew can control the pulpit ... People have many needs and wants, and they put pressure on the preacher to fit in with their particular need, how they see the world, and what the world wants and needs.'[49] Yes, heaven forbid that we should take any notice of their needs or wants. What do they think this is, a democracy?

Look, it's a false dichotomy. It's not a question of choosing between 'the gospel' on the one hand and 'the needs of the pew' on the other. Both should be addressed.

Relevance. It's a Marmite word, you either love it or hate it, with no in-betweens. Quite why people react so strongly to it is a mystery. It seems rather obvious that the teaching has to be relevant to the needs of the congregation – otherwise why bother to listen? After all, wherever we go to learn, we need stuff that is relevant to us. If you went to Bible College and they taught you zoology, you might want your money back.[*]

Perhaps the problem is that making your teaching relevant, by its nature, involves listening to your congregation. And that is what worries an awful lot of preachers. We like speaking, we don't like listening. My beloved wife™ once gave me a birthday card with a picture of an old Victorian gent, and the phrase 'Everyone is entitled to the benefit of my opinions.' This more or less sums up a lot of preaching styles. 'We're here to *give* opinions, not listen to them; we're here to proclaim, not discuss; we're here to provide answers, not encourage questions. I'll be the judge of what's relevant, thank you very much.'

This is not what Jesus did. He marched into peoples' lives, had a good nose around and started to ask them questions. If anyone's teaching was ever relevant, then surely his was. As we've seen, his teaching in the gospels was nearly always in response to questions. People came up to him and tested him, or asked him things that were concerning them, or poured out their hearts to him and he responded.

'Should we pay taxes to Caesar?'

'What should I do to inherit eternal life?'

---

[*] Or you might turn into a fantastic vet - but it's unlikely.

'Is it permissible to heal on the Sabbath?'

They asked. He answered. And he used those answers as a launchpad to take people into whole new areas. Ask, apparently, and it shall be given to you.

The road has moved

Just near where we live there is a church in the middle of a field. It's a small church and quite a big field and you have to go to some lengths to make it across to the building.

When we first saw it, we wondered who on earth had put it there. The road wasn't that far away, why build your church in a field? Then we discovered that under the floor of the church were the remains of an old Roman villa, which originally stood by the road. As the centuries went by, the road moved, but the church stayed where it was. The result is that the church stands there, picturesque but isolated.

You can stand in splendid isolation if you like. You can ignore the reality of people's lives and stay put in the place you have always been. You might create sermons of beauty, of power, of holiness.

But you'll still be on your own, in a field.

Anyone seen the road?

Remedies for short-sightedness

Understand their world

Jesus was sensitive to his audience. His stories worked because they reflected the world of his audience – tales of farmers and builders and vineyards and weddings – tales about the kingdom of God told in the language of first century Palestine. He was able to do this, however, because he had put in the hard work. There is no shortcut to this; Jesus didn't parachute in at the age of thirty and start talking to people. He lived in Nazareth for some twenty-five years before he began to tell his stories. He worked on the building sites of Galilee. He shared in the life of a small village community. He saw their anger and tears and sweat, their hope and hatred, their joy and love.

> Introduce an idea we can easily relate to and nod sympathetically.

Incarnation. Living among people. Being part of the culture, not aloof from it. This, above all, is what enables us to engage with people and to see the possibilities they hold. It allows us to borrow their glasses, and see the world through their eyes.

How much do you know about the world of your congregation? How much do you know about their jobs, their hobbies, their families – not to mention their hopes, their fears, their problems...

Get out of the field

It's been said that a preacher should prepare with the Bible in one hand and the newspaper in the other.* These days, however, it feels like a good preacher could also do with watching the internet, while balancing a novel on one foot and a DVD player on the other.

This is not just about being relevant. It's about fuelling your sermons, feeding them with stories and images, ideas and metaphors. The point is that preaching needs to develop a wide vision: we need to look at the world around us.

Sermons which have too narrow a focus, which fail to engage with the world around them, are mere theoretical activities. If you want to go back to the argument about prophets, you have to admit that the prophets were

---

* Although who said it, is not so certain: it's been variously attributed to Spurgeon, Karl Barth and John Stott!

nothing if not politically relevant: they were often passionately concerned with the politics of their time.

> *Engage with the secular to link to our spiritual lives – secular music/film/tv.*

A wider view of the world keeps us from focusing only on our own issues and problems. The Church does have a tendency to drift away from real life. It means that some issues which are of huge concern – work, for instance – are rarely addressed. In a 1997 survey, Mark Greene rated sermons on a helpfulness scale of 0-4. He found that sermons were rated helpful in the following areas:

- Personal life: 2.6
- Church life: 2.1
- Home life: 1.8
- Work life: 1.7

He concluded that 'the further a Christian gets from the church building, the less likely they are to have an adequate base of teaching to lead lives in a godly manner.'[50]

> *How do I advance my career and my income ... deal with conflict with friends, family, work ... debt, unemployment, stress, dating, sex, depression, loneliness, boredom, time?*

We all need help to reflect biblically on the world around us. Jesus was a political preacher. His teaching and his life were a direct challenge to the powers around him. (After all, Pilate had Jesus killed for political reasons, not for theological ones.) His stories, even, make political references. The parable of the talents begins 'A nobleman went to a distant country to get royal power for himself and then return...'[51] Both Herod the Great and his son Archelaus had to travel to Rome before their power was confirmed. (Herod got to be called 'King', his son had the lesser title of 'Ethnarch'.)

The man in Jesus' parable goes off on his journey, but the story continues: 'But the citizens of his country hated him and sent a delegation after him, saying, "We do not want this man to rule over us."[52] This is a clear reference to a topical event, an allusion to the delegation that went to Rome to try to stop Augustus confirming Archelaus as ruler of Judea. In other words, Jesus has taken a contemporary political event and used it as the basis for a parable.[53]

Find me the metaphor

Taking a wider view will resource your preaching, because it will provide you with stories, poems, art, anecdote, quotes and a whole battery of illustrations to add to your teaching.

Some people are natural raconteurs who can take the events of their lives and weave them into all kinds of weird and wonderful stories. Others have to look around. But the newspaper is a great source of stories. Read it and ask yourself, what point could I draw out of this? It may fit perfectly with the message you are preaching, which is great, but if it doesn't, keep the clipping and store the story for future reference.

Keep a notebook or journal with ideas and resources for your preaching: stories you've heard, passages you've read. Learn to look around. The wider your reading, the richer your preaching. The better engaged you are with contemporary culture, the more connections you will be able to make with your congregation. You can draw your metaphors, stories and illustrations from science and arts, from sport and the movies. Just get out there and keep your eyes open.

Culturewatch is a web resource produced by Damaris, a Christian organisation, to help people explore the message behind the media (www. damaris.org). It includes tons of up-to-date resources on books, films, music, television, art and theatre – and, if you want, you can request a weekly update.

Face the problems

Consider your congregation. Perhaps the issue they are struggling with is that of anger – they have come to church this morning having just about held themselves back from clocking their son, or even their wife or husband. They feel inside themselves a constant battle to keep their temper in check, to control their tongue or their fists.

Or perhaps they are scared – of losing their job, their home or their partner. They want to know if there is a solution to their problems. But they are at the whim of a teaching syllabus which has been designed without any consultation. They might wait years before hearing a sermon on a subject that really matters to them. And all the time, the white noise of their problems is drowning out the voice of the speaker.

> The task is to facilitate for each person an encounter with the living God, by whatever means the Holy Spirit suggests. This is rarely a three point monologue.

Acknowledging those problems and allowing space for teaching and discussion of them will diffuse the frustration of some of your listeners and build up those who might need to store the knowledge for another day.[54]

The elephant in the pews

If you've been through theology college, you may have spent a lot of time answering crucial and difficult questions (or deciding that they can't be answered). But the people in church may still be facing those issues; they may have different perspectives and more down to earth questions.

For example, in sermons about Abraham sacrificing Isaac, we may well want to emphasise the faith of Abraham.[55] But that is not likely to be the first question that the congregation is asking. They're thinking 'Huh? How could God ask that of anyone?' or 'How could Abraham possibly go along with this?' There is often, as it were, an elephant in the pews, a huge and basic question that needs to be dealt with – particularly in Old Testament passages which come from a culture and a time very different to our own. Those 'basic' questions need to be acknowledged. If you are not going to deal with them in any depth, then there needs to be a place where they can be parked, so that the congregation can concentrate on what you *are* going to say.

If you don't know what the real questions are, then you could always ask them. You could set up a mailbox at the back of the church to receive questions, or give people ten minutes to write their questions on a flipchart. Or you could set up a question and answer event. Recently, to accompany a sermon series on Revelation at our church, we set up an evening of question and answers. Called *Apocalypse Now*, the idea was to give background information about the book and to encourage people to ask questions of the people who were preaching the series. Evenings like this also force the preachers to be on their toes!

You need, in short, to deal with the big, obvious problem or question about the passage – the elephant in the pews. Otherwise all it does is block everyone's view.

Lose the jargon

If we don't know who we're talking to, we won't know how to talk to them.

It's like when I talk to my kids about a record player. They look at me as though I were speaking Swahili.[*] And yet we routinely pepper our sermons with words and phrases which the unchurched would find bafflingly incomprehensible. As Craddock puts it, 'the church has no retirement program for old words that fought well at Nicaea, Chalcedon and Augsburg; they are kept in the line of march even if the whole mission is slowed to a snail's pace and observers on the side are bent double with laughter.'[56]

It's not that all our words ought, or even need, to go: what has to change is the assumption that everyone in the church knows what we mean. Too often we simply repeat jargon which has no connection with the listener. And then we blame them for not listening.

> I would like to be able to put my hand up and ask when I don't understand their vocabulary or their point.

(One of the most baffling things about writing this book has been trying to wade through the swamp of theological jargon. Books on preaching – or 'homiletical literature' – are some of the most impenetrably written books in the world. For an art which is trying to communicate with ordinary people, one suspects that someone is missing the point.)

---

[*] I spoke Swahili to them the other day. They thought I was talking about a record player.

Speak their language

One of the greatest sermons ever is not a real sermon at all. Or, at least, not one that was ever actually preached. It comes from Herman Melville's novel, *Moby Dick*, and it's the perfect illustration of a sermon which is totally grounded in the language and culture of the listeners. The hero, Ishmael, goes to church, where he hears a sermon by Father Mapple, a former sailor and harpooner, turned Christian minister. Everything in Mapple's church – even the surroundings – is focused on his audience: the mariners and whalers of New Bedford. His pulpit is shaped in 'the likeness of a ship's bluff bows' and is reached by means of a rope ladder, which Mapple hauls up after him. His sermon – on Jonah, of course – is crammed with nautical terms

> *Shipmates, this book, containing only four chapters – four yarns – is one of the smallest strands in the mighty cable of the Scriptures. Yet what depths of the soul Jonah's deep sealine sound! What a pregnant lesson to us is this prophet! What a noble thing is that canticle in the fish's belly! How billow-like and boisterously grand! We feel the floods surging over us, we sound with him to the kelpy bottom of the waters; sea-weed and all the slime of the sea is about us! But what is this lesson that the book of Jonah teaches? Shipmates, it is a two-stranded lesson; a lesson to us all as sinful men, and a lesson to me as a pilot of the living God...*[57]

The interesting thing is that Mapple is actually based on real preachers whom Melville had seen and heard, particularly Edward Taylor of the Boston Bethel, whose nautically-themed sermons became something of a tourist attraction.

Taylor was described by Charles Dickens as someone who 'addresses himself peculiarly to seamen, and who was once a mariner himself' and who, although eccentric, 'studied their [his listeners'] sympathies and understandings much more than the display of his own powers. His imagery was all drawn from the sea, and from the incidents of a seaman's life; and was often remarkably good.'[58]

Spurgeon also said of Taylor that, 'No ideas of propriety, or notions of delicacy, hung about him like fetters: he spoke to sailors, not to squeamish pomposity's [sic]'[*]

Perhaps one of the best exponents of understanding culture and language was Martin Luther (1483–1546). The use of the vernacular was crucial to Luther's success. He translated the Scriptures into the language of the German people – the real German people, the ones in the marketplace and the street. His sermons have a sense of life and death. Full of vibrant, earthy language, they are, at times, extraordinarily vulgar and even crude.[**] We're not suggesting you go that far! But you could take a leaf out of Luther's book at times and listen to the language people use and the way they speak. Luther may have been potty-mouthed, but he knew his people and he spoke their language. And they listened.

For preaching team meetings or personal reflection

1. Meet at someone's place of work to help think through how a sermon series could be relevant to people working there.

2. Invite someone along to talk about how to welcome and include everyone. Discuss how to make things better and appoint two people to take action.

3. Challenge people to visit a part of their community they normally don't go to. (Go in pairs if it requires courage!)

> Be aware of the single people in their twenties, thirties, forties, fifties, sixties, etc – we are not to be treated with things that are primarily for kids, youth or families. This alienates us – WE HAVE OUR OWN STRUGGLES!!

---

[*] *Eccentric Preachers*, Spurgeon. The chapter on Taylor can be found at: http://www.spurgeon.org/misc/ep12.htm. Taylor was not known for respect for authority. A noted pillar of the community once came in to a prayer meeting and made a speech telling everyone how grateful they should be for the way that the rich people of the town had helped these poor degraded sailors. As soon as he'd finished, Taylor stood up and asked, 'Is there any other old sinner from up town who would like to say a word before we go on with the meeting?'

[**] As this is a family book we decided not to put any examples in. But if you want to find out more, there's a quote on the website.

GREAT MOMENTS IN PREACHING
No.5 – LUTHER PREACHES TO THE PEASANTS

Problems with the content

Complaint 5: The sermon is hard of hearing

Talking of listening... Many churches have a loop system to help their congregation hear. Sadly, the loop doesn't always make it all the way round and back to the preacher.

In some churches there is a lot of frustration because the preachers just don't seem to be listening to the congregation. Our listeners may want to say something about the sermon, but there is no 'official' way for them to be heard. There is seldom a proper mechanism to enable the congregation to comment or respond, a structured way of giving feedback.

Now, we know that as soon as we mention the word 'feedback' many preachers will start to laugh bitterly and want to go and lie down in a darkened room. That's because much of 'Christian' feedback consists of a member of the congregation saying something like 'About your sermon, Vicar...' before tearing it into little pieces. So, for many ministers, their experience of feedback is akin to being charged and gored by a three ton bull. On steroids.

But if people are given no structured way to comment, then they will take an unstructured way. If they feel no-one is listening, they will end up shouting. And, let's face it, they have a right to be heard. When the sermon series on the siege of Jerusalem feels worse than the actual siege itself, someone is going to get hurt. As Doug Pagitt writes: 'Being part of a church for twelve years and hearing the thoughts some six hundred times, but never having the pastor hear you, is a dangerous imbalance of power.'[59]

Feedback, painful though it might be at times, can be a friend. A Jewish story tells of Aaron the Tanner. A thoughtful, educated man, he was deeply versed in the Scriptures, so much so that he used to constantly criticise the decisions of a famous rabbi and pick up errors and inconsistencies in his sermons. When Aaron died, people saw it as a judgment on him for all these criticisms. Yet on the day of Aaron's funeral, the rabbi – the target of his criticism – was found weeping and sobbing with grief. 'Why do you weep?' they asked him. 'He was always correcting you. He was always criticising you and picking you to pieces!' 'Exactly,' replied the rabbi. 'He was my truest friend. He forced me to think clearly and reason carefully. Who is going to show me my faults now?'

Remedies for deafness

Feedback from your congregation

There are loads of ways to do good, structured feedback – but they won't happen by themselves. We offer some suggestions below – but it's up to you to take the initiative and find the best way for you and your church to dialogue.

Your 'hearing aid' could be a suggestion box at the back of the church. You could ask people for responses to past sermons, or suggest issues or passages from the Bible for future sermons. Or you could offer a range of topics and ask people to choose which ones would be helpful.

It could be an email. When planning a sermon, it might be worth sending the passage out to a number of people and asking them some key questions on the subject. For instance, in preparation for a short talk on prayer, our vicar emailed ten people with the following three questions:

- What is prayer to you?
- How often do you pray?
- What is difficult about praying?

From the answers he received, he constructed his talk.

It could be a meeting. Some churches have a forum for staff to feedback on sermons, which can be very helpful. But we need to ask our listeners as well: are our stories hitting the mark? Are personal affectations getting in the way of the message? Is the topic explained clearly enough?

It could be a chat with one or more people over a pint. It's that easy.

It comes down to how we view people. If we see them as sheep to be herded, we won't take much notice of their points of view. But if we see them as friends, family, travelling companions, then iron will sharpen iron, and their advice will make us better teachers.

Catherine Frieze and Anne Vautrey are Methodist preachers on the Leeds North East Circuit. After one particular local preachers meeting, they say, the discussion 'sparked us off wanting to learn more about the twelve congregations we serve. We decided to go out in pairs to have a structured conversation with representatives from each congregation. We wanted a common approach. What was uncommon was that the preachers were doing more of the listening and the worshippers were doing more of the talking!'[60]

Feedback from your colleagues

Every trainee minister undergoes preaching classes while in college, where their sermons are scrutinized and critiqued. But after they leave? What happens then?

How are local ministers passing on their knowledge about preaching to others? It's a question I ask every trainee minister before they leave college: 'How will you pass on what you have learnt?'

Some of them are clear about what they'll do. Some are still getting it together themselves. Some feel tentative about the 'how' and 'when' of talking about someone else's sermon.

One obvious way is to use your preaching team. If the group feels awkward about giving feedback, perhaps what is needed is a good system: a simple reflection journal that charts the journey and provides the questions that they dare not ask. Possible resources include:

- *Your Way with God's Word* by David J. Schlafer is fairly exhaustive and sometimes rather off the wall, but very creative and would provide enough questions to last you a lifetime!
- *Surviving the Sermon,* also by David Schlafer, has good questions at the back.
- *A Preaching Workbook* by David Day would provide a good starting place. Despite not exactly being a workbook (there's no space to write in it) it could provide a stimulus for creating a preaching journal of your own.
- *Developing Reflective Practice for Preachers* by Charles Chadwick & Phillip Tovey (Grove Booklets) would also get people talking – and it wouldn't cost too much to supply every member of the preaching team with a copy.

If your church receives trainee ministers, it makes sense to extend the system that is used with them – feedback sheets, discussions – to the preaching team. Ministerial students could sometimes reflect within the forum of the preaching team meeting, and this might open up areas that are difficult to discuss with senior, lay or retired preachers.

Bill Hybels, pastor of Willow Creek Community Church in Barrington, Illinois, describes how he collaborates with his elders and lets them critique his sermons. Originally he found that unless he asked them, they would not venture a critique. So now he has a more formal process

Now the elders evaluate every message that I preach, and they give me a written response to it within minutes after I complete the message. One elder – our most discerning when it comes to preaching evaluation – collects responses from the other elders, summarizes them, and writes them on the front of a bulletin and gives it to me before I leave.

Hybels adds that the process only works because of the love and trust between them as a group

When I work sometimes twenty-five or thirty hours on a sermon, I pour my life into it, pray over it, and write out three drafts. If the evaluation were not done with great sensitivity and with no ulterior motives from the evaluators, the system would be imperiled.[61]

Of course, you may not be in charge of the preaching team meetings, but you can pick and choose from these possibilities and suggest them to your group. We're going to have to invest in people with time, training and, probably, money, if we want to see a change in culture. Look out for training days that will inspire people and help them gain new skills.

And remember, the most important part of feedback is the opening statement. If you charge straight in, it puts people on the defensive straight away. Look for the positives and sprinkle them liberally throughout your feedback. Too much negativity is destructive, not constructive. This is iron sharpening iron, not a swordfight.

For preaching team meetings or personal reflection

1. Discuss how you would fit a time for questions into your sermons.
2. Ask for written feedback from members of the congregation on a sermon by each preacher on the team (at least once per year) and discuss.
3. Create 'preaching buddies' – pairs of preachers who will listen to each others' sermons and informally mentor one another. You could use the CPAS 'Growing Leaders' course as a structure for this.

Problems with the content

Complaint 6: The sermon is rambling and confused

There was a craze some time ago for those magic pictures. These were abstract-looking pieces of art which turned into 3-D images if you stared at them from the right angle, or blurred your eyes a bit. You thought it was just a squiggle of colour, but if you just lost focus enough – hey presto! It was three dolphins juggling a beach ball!

Many sermons are like that. Only without the dolphins.

You sit there thinking, 'This looks like a shapeless mess, but surely if I just blur my vision, if I try *really* hard I should be able to get the overall picture ... nope. Lost it again.'

The ramblers society

The sermon is confused and so are many of its listeners. It can't remember why it's here, where it's going, or what it's supposed to be doing. It's all right for the person doing the preaching: they've got a script, or some kind of notes (even though they might be in the wrong order). The rest of the congregation has just got to hang in there, hoping that all this meandering is actually leading somewhere and trying to guess the overall shape. Unless your church is blessed enough to have Powerpoint, you can waste a lot of energy trying to guess where the preacher is going next. Actually, even if you do have PowerPoint, you might still be wasting a lot of energy.

So, although preachers are frequently taught structures (e.g. the ubiquitous three-point sermon) there is still scope for plenty of confusion. Individual sections might make sense, the odd story might threaten some kind of meaning, but there's no straight line.

And how often have you sat in a sermon, waiting for some kind of conclusion, only for the thing to end abruptly, like an art house film where everyone leaves the cinema rubbing their eyes and saying to each other, 'Now what was *that* all about?'

What is true of the individual sermon is also often true of the sermon series, with precious little connection between one week and the next. Or there may be no series at all, except the lectionary – and you need a degree in mathematics to understand that. Certainly there is rarely a sense of revising what's been learned or checking what's been missed. It's possible that the people on the preaching rota are no more than a ramblers society.

A nasty swelling

If you haven't struck oil, stop boring.

On 24th April, the Ship of Fools website sent seventy of its crack 'Mystery Worshippers' off to churches throughout London. Their mission? To check out the length and health of the capital's sermons.

The results were interesting.

The longest sermons were delivered at some of London's major and most well-known churches: eighty minutes at Hyde Park (in French), fifty-three minutes at the Dominion Theatre on Tottenham Court Road and fifty-two minutes at Westminster Chapel, Buckingham Gate. (At the latter, the Mystery Worshipper, known only as 'Hurdy Gurdy', reported that 'The preacher said some good stuff but I kept checking my watch and began praying for the end. At least it got me praying.')

Six of the top ten shortest sermons were delivered in Anglican services. The average sermon length across all the churches visited was twenty minutes thirty-one seconds. If you'd gone to Westminster or St Paul's Cathedral that day, you would have got off lightly. No sermons there.

> Don't go on and on and on – our attention spans are not very large.

Most sermons are simply too long. (And here, I pause, so that anyone who knows me, or has ever heard me preach, can indulge themselves with a bout of hysterical laughter.)

I know the excuses. It's pretty hard to keep track of time while preaching. And sometimes people seem rather too concerned with time-keeping. For example, this appeared on one of our comment cards:

> In the good British tradition my lunch is at 1 o'clock. And grandfather taught me never to be late.

We're not suggesting that the length of the sermon should be the most important factor. Lunch can wait – say what you feel you have to say. But when you start to say a lot more than is necessary, when the sermon becomes too drawn-out or digressive, then the smell of the roast potatoes threatens to overpower your message.

Keeping anything short – sermons, books, visits to the pub – can be tricky. There is always so much you want to say, that cutting it down is hard. And sometimes it comes down to confidence, that you have said what you wanted to say.

> *After twenty minutes you've lost me, unless you're very, very good.*

A friend of mine who is an excellent, inspirational speaker, and certainly not known for the brevity of his talks, made the move to motivational speaking for businesses. When I asked him what the biggest change was, he replied, 'Time. In business, if you've gone over ten minutes, they think you've gone on for too long.' Needless to say, for someone used to speaking on stage at big Christian events, ten minutes was nothing!

But sometimes, if we're honest, we plod on with our talk when it should have been put out of its misery long before. You know all's not well, but you keep going in the hope that some miracle will suddenly make it all right. It doesn't. People simply switch off. They start to do other things. They check their diary, or look up obscure Bible passages to pass the time, or write notes about something else entirely, whilst trying to look like they're taking notes on the sermon.

Look at the size of my exegesis!

One of the chief problems is that preachers confuse output with outcome.

Output means the stuff that you do, the products or services produced. It's a measure of activity. In communication terms it might be the number of press releases you've sent out, the number of leaflets distributed, or phone calls made. Outcome, however, is the effects or changes that result from the output. Outcome is whether people's understanding or attitudes

GREAT MOMENTS IN PREACHING
No.6 – ERASMUS TRANSLATES THE GREEK NEW TESTAMENT

What's Greek for 'Hummus'?

have been changed by those press releases, whether all those leaflets resulted in people buying your product, whether those phone calls made new customers. Output is activity; outcome is productivity.

In church terms, we often measure things by output. We count the number of people in the service, or the hours spent on sermon preparation, or the minutes preached. But those are irrelevant, if there's no outcome. It doesn't matter how many hours you've spent poring over the commentaries or translating the passage anew from the Greek. The Puritan preacher Samuel Torshell thought it bad preaching to 'tell you how many Fathers we have read, how much we are acquainted with the schoolmen, what critical linguists we are or the like. It is a wretched ostentation.' While Jeremiah Dyke aimed to 'make our people scholars', rather than 'show ourselves scholars to our people'.[62]

A church of one hundred people who go home and do nothing for the kingdom is worse than a church of three people who are living for Jesus. A sermon which took ten hours to prepare and which bored people to death is worse than one which took ten minutes and changed someone's life.[*]

Longer is not better, it's just longer. It's just more output.

Remedies for confusion and rambling

Walk the line

> *Have a clear structure, bearing in mind what you want me to take away.*

All teachers have to produce lesson plans. These tell you the starting point, the desired outcome of the lesson and the line – the path along which the lesson will proceed in order to get to the destination.

You should have a sermon plan. Start with where your congregation are and end with where you want them to be.

Now envisage your sermon as a line. Each part of the sermon should move you further along that line. You can make occasional diversions from the line, but not for long. Otherwise, you'll get lost.

A lesson plan has four main elements:

- The destination – what students will learn, what they will be able to do as a result of the lesson.

- The starting point – what they already know, their status at the beginning of the lesson.

- The content – and how you're going to assist them in learning the new material. This includes not only input from the teacher, but

---

[*] The Bible is full of exhortations to consider outcome rather than output. Amos 5:21-24 is all about this. The priests measured the festivals, the assemblies, the amount of offerings, the volume of their songs – but there was no outcome. There was no justice.

the practice which the students will do to try out their new skills or work with new ideas.

- Evaluation – how you will evaluate whether or not they've learned it.

The plan will also list other items, such as the title of the lesson, the time required to complete it, a list of required materials and homework.

The lesson plan is a basic tool of the teacher's trade. Millions of hours of teaching have led teaching professionals to the conclusion that a lesson plan is vital. Now, when was the last time preachers did a similar thing for the sermon?

Oh.

Ask: so what?

The single most important question you can ask about a sermon is: so what? What difference does this sermon make to people's lives? What do they get out of it? You may find your three part series on 'Philistine Foreign Policy in the Age of Hezekiah' absolutely fascinating, but what are you asking people to do as a result? What difference does it make to your congregation?

In order for anyone to be motivated to learn, their brain needs to find a meaningful benefit. Our dog, Bill, needs to know there'll be a treat if he comes when called.* You may have never thought about what the meaningful benefit of your sermon is, still less tried to articulate it, but if it's not there, the congregation will be left wondering why they bothered to listen.

Kathy Sierra suggests playing the 'Why? Who Cares? So What?' game in order to discover the 'meaningful benefit' of any piece of learning. In this instance, the way it would work would be for you to sit down with a friend or relation and try describing the content of your sermon in a nutshell to them. Get them to ask you 'Why?' You give them an answer. They ask you 'Who cares?' You give your answer. They ask 'So what?'

'At this point,' she says, 'when you're nearly ready to kill them for not getting it, you probably have the thing you should have said, instead of whatever you said first (and second). The most compelling and motivating reason/benefit is almost always the thing you say only after you've answered at least three "Yeah, but WHY do I care?" questions.'[63]

---

* Nick works along broadly similar lines.

It helps to talk it through with someone else. If you share your thoughts with your friend/colleague/psychiatrist/salsa partner they might be able to help you simplify and clarify the structure of your sermon. When their eyes glaze over and they fall face first into their soup, you'll be able to spot the bits which you think are fascinating, but they fail to find so riveting.

Read all about it

In the last thirty years, many inspiring books have been written about the style and structure of the sermon. From puritan plain style to genre-based preaching and first person narrative; from deductive to inductive, from Paul Scott Wilson's *Four Pages of the Preacher* to Buttrick's *Plot and Moves*, from itch to scratch, from Oops to Yeah; there's never been more help in finding new ways to shape and structure what you want to say.

What was the last book you read on preaching style? And did you try out any of the suggestions? Even those who regularly preach read a shockingly small amount on the subject, and although you won't find these books in your local library, they're only a Google away. I've read a lot of books on style and structure in recent months (although probably only a small percentage of it, as it's quite an industry now) and not all of it is very readable, but even the less digestible stuff is seminal. A lot of people have done a lot of the thinking, trialling and reviewing of preaching styles for you.

For preaching team meetings or personal reflection

1. Share sample sermon plans.
2. Working as individuals, pairs or in groups, plan a sermon outline for a specific occasion, e.g. All Age Worship. Then allow an extra ten minutes to write the first paragraph. Each person or group should present something. Play the 'So what' game as part of this.
3. Agree to read a book on sermon structure and share your thoughts and opinions on it at a later meeting.

Problems with the presentation

Complaint 7: The sermon lacks energy

A few years ago, ITV's *South Bank Show* featured the work of Red Priest, a baroque music group. Unlike most orchestras and ensembles, they play from memory, which means they can act and interact with one another and the audience. Compare that to the static performance of a symphony orchestra. People might arrive to the Festival Hall buzzing with energy and excitement but after a few minutes with nothing to watch and limited eye contact, the audience's eyes begin to glaze over. The orchestra sits heads down, eyes on the sheet music and doesn't look up at the audience till the performance ends.[64]

Now think about the local church: the harbinger of abundant life, but too often dressed in black, not moving, and reading from a script. The preacher, reliant on a sermon script, might be playing the music correctly, but with no sign of life. Nothing is more deadening than hearing a preacher read their sermon from a script.

> The habit of writing out and reading full sermons in the pulpit ... is largely responsible for our having lost sight of the importance of having a single well-defined statement around which the entire sermon is constructed. Essays are, by their nature, complicated statements. Sermons, preached without notes, by their nature, cannot be complicated statements. Essays are meant to be read in private as words on a page; sermons are meant to be heard as spoken events.[65]

If you arrived at the theatre for a Shakespeare play, and the actors just stood and read from their copies of the Arden text, with footnotes, you'd want your money back. People want something to watch as well – something visual that makes a connection, something to take to heart, something that remains once the show is over.

Please could you preach and teach from your heart and from what's inside you (provided, of course, that the message is biblically-based) rather than read a carefully constructed essay, which is often so lifeless and boring.

Remedies for lack of energy

Here are some simple ways to make your sermon more lively.

Ditch the script

Don't refer too much to notes – don't read your sermon – paper is not a good conductor of heat.

This is the first step to more memorable sermons. And it will make you a better speaker as well. According to Toastmasters International, one of the ten biggest public speaking mistakes is 'Reading a Speech Word for Word' which will 'put the audience to sleep'.

Preaching without a script will not just add dynamism to your sermon, it will make it more memorable. Why? Because you will have remembered it yourself. (So at least one person will be able to talk about it afterwards!) The point is, if you can't tell people what they need to know without looking at a piece of paper, how do you expect them to remember, still less to tell anyone else?

This may be a big step, and we don't necessarily advise you do without any notes whatsoever. What we're recommending is that you ditch the fully-scripted sermon. Have your main headings, by all means. Note down your illustrations or any quotes you're going to use. But don't write an essay and then read the thing out. Look at Spurgeon's preaching notes at the beginning of this book if you want an example![*]

Freeing yourself from the script will add so much: it will enable you to move around, it will change the dynamic between you and the audience. If you're not looking at a script, you'll be able to see the response in their eyes.

So ditch the script and play from memory. It adds life and energy and people are far more likely to leave humming the tune.

Improve your wossname ... thingy, you know – memory

But you might be daunted by the idea of memorising your talk. Well, there are four things that will help your memory improve:

---

[*] Opposite the 'Before we begin' page.

1. Get fit – you can't do a good job without a healthy mind and body, so eat well, pay attention to your fitness regime, walk lots, dance too, and get enough sleep!

2. Find the thing that zings within the subject matter that you're expected to talk about. Find the thing that really interests you. You will remember what really matters to you.

3. Build a framework – structuring your speech helps you remember what to say. If you organise your material clearly and concisely, that's half the battle. Often we just think that amassing what we have to say is enough, but the next stage, where you break your talk up into chunks, is what helps you and the listener to think clearly. There are numerous ways of doing this (see *Patterns of Preaching* by Ronald J. Allen) but the important thing is to do it in good time. Deciding on headings and subheadings will help you as you memorise what you want to say.

4. Talk to yourself – in other words, practise memorising your talk before you give it. Keep in shape by exercising your memory in other ways, too. You have got to put some effort in. If you build up your strength in the gym, you'll have strength to do the jobs you need to do outside. Flexing your memory muscles in other situations, e.g. remembering a message, or learning a list, or a poem, just for fun, will train your memory muscles not to let you down in front of others.

This will have so many other benefits. In fact, we'd go so far as to say that preaching without notes is *the single most important thing you can do to improve your sermons*.

PRACTISE!

Once you can put your notes down, and remember what you were going to say, you'll also be able to move more. You won't be dependent on the preacher's zimmer frame – the lectern – you will be free to speak and teach like a human being, rather than an automaton. You will be able to look into people's eyes and talk from the heart, which means that the way you speak will change. Your voice will naturally and more freely use a greater variety of inflections that people will recognise as conversational in tone. You will be able to genuinely enthuse, inspire, corral and confront people with the challenges of God's call. And they, for their part, will happily sit up and listen, engage, discuss and possibly, even, do what you're asking them to do. And all because you got your memory moving.

Cut it out!

Another benefit of memorising your sermon is that it will pare the sermon down to its core essentials. You're always more likely to over-write than over-remember! Asking the 'So what' question will help as well, because it will force you to concentrate on the main message.

There are no hard and fast rules about sermon length. Short sermons are not automatically more interesting. (However, they are over quicker.) The key thing is to work out how much time you need and don't pad it out. Don't feel you have to fill the slot. And it is undoubtedly true that the longer you talk, the harder it is to keep people's attention. So don't be greedy with people's time. They have come to church, out of busy lives, and given you their attention. Don't waste it.

Stick to the readings – don't stray from the point.

For preaching team meetings or personal reflection

1. Put people in teams and quiz them on areas where the team needs to improve, e.g. learning the names of the congregation or going through the vocal checklist. Give a prize for the best answers.

2. See if you can recall last Sunday's sermon outline.

3. Ask the person preaching the next sermon to give a short version of it without notes.

Problems with the presentation

Complaint 8: The sermon lacks mobility

A lot of preaching is static. There are few gestures and little freedom. The preacher in the pulpit clearly is confined. But, as we have seen, the preacher on the platform is often no less so, tied to the lectern, often clinging to it like a drowning man holding on to a lifebelt.

The effect is, well, *boring*. In a world where people are used to a lot of visual input, standing still is probably the least visual thing that a preacher can do. (Especially if wearing a grey suit.) You could achieve the same effect by putting a mannequin up front and playing a recording. Or shutting your eyes and pretending you're listening to Radio 4. Either way, it doesn't seem to convey much Abundant and Everlasting Life – when that's the very message we're trying to convey.

When you stand up in church, people see you in 3-D. You are a complete body. In that way, being in church is like being in the theatre. We read your body as well as your words – the way you stand, the way you move – they all tell us something about you, your relation to us and to what you are saying. Are you rooted to the spot? Can you even look up? Dare you move away from your notes? And, if you do, do you know what to do with your hands? All these things can reduce your VPL – your Visible Preaching Line – so that people take more notice of what you say, than the way that you say it.

The answer to many of the sermon's problems – poor mobility, stasis, dullness – is exercise: for the muscles, the memory, and the imagination.

Remedies for immobility

Record yourself

You need to be aware of what the picture looks like for the people looking at you. This is why watching a recording of yourself can be so enlightening. You might be completely dwarfed by a huge stained glass window behind you or any number of competing distractions. You might be in shadow. You might look like you're giving a lecture, when you want it to be more of a conversation. Maybe you think people should care only about the word being preached and shouldn't notice all this peripheral stuff. But they do. These things are important. And if you show that you are sensitive to other people's viewpoints – that is a big plus.

Get out of the pulpit

The word 'pulpit' comes from the Latin *pulpitum* which means 'platform or stage'.[*] Pulpits are not that ancient. They date back to the Middle Ages. Before that, either the bishop preached from his *cathedra* – his chair or throne (hence the phrase *ex cathedra* – from the throne) or clergy preached from a simple raised platform called an *ambo*.[66]

As the status of the sermon rose in the Middle Ages, the pulpit rose with it. This was more than a device to help people be seen and heard: it was a symbol of the importance of the sermon and the separateness of the preacher. He was raised above his congregation and kept apart from them. As time went by, many pulpits became richly and ornately decorated. Sometimes they would be decorated with the great figures of the Bible – Moses, the apostles, Jesus Christ – to show that the preacher stood in the line of apostolic and biblical authority.

GREAT MOMENTS IN PREACHING
No.7 – THE WORLD'S SMALLEST PREACHER DISCOVERS THE PULPIT'S DESIGN FLAW

Anyone there?

---

* It also means scaffold. Draw your own conclusions.

As we've already said, that idea of authority has changed. As Craddock points out

> *Unfortunately, the physical arrangements for preaching make it difficult for the minister to implement the changed relation between speaker and hearer. The very location and elevation of the pulpit imply an authority on the part of the speaker or the message that the minister is hesitant to assume and the listeners no longer recognise.*[67]

Listeners no longer sign up to the idea that the pulpit confers a special authority. You don't need it to be seen or heard any more (not that it was ever really about that anyway). You don't need to rise above your congregation. Get out and move around. If you stay in the pulpit, all you'll give people is a pain in the neck.

Stand still

Do try to vary voice tone and don't move around too much!

As well as knowing how to move, it's important to have good posture and to be able to stand still. Now this may sound like a contradiction of what's been said before, but it's not. It's great to have energy and dynamism, but it's not great if you move about so much that everyone feels seasick. In between purposeful determined movement, there needs to be stillness.

Try it now. It's obviously easier when you're sitting down with no one watching you. But when all eyes are looking in your direction, as if you are a picture to be studied, you realise how difficult it is. Especially your hands. Suddenly they feel huge and without vocation. What on earth does one do with them? Feet want to fidget, fingers want to fiddle. But the body is transparent. Even when our words are smooth and our smile is fixed, our nerves or excitement still reveal themselves through toes that tap, shoulders that wriggle and hips that sway.

Standing still shouldn't mean your knees are permanently locked and your feet are cemented to the ground. It just means that your use of movement needs to be purposeful and judicious, rather than ever roaming like a hungry dog. In between times, stand still and let the eye rest. Imagine yourself, standing with confidence and ease before your Creator, carrying nothing, waiting on His word. Can you do it?

Get up, out of your chair, and do the 'standing still exercise':

- Place your feet apart, the width of your shoulders
- Pull yourself up to your full height, lifting the ribcage out of your waist (you'll lose pounds in moments!) – picture the vertebrae sitting one on top of the other
- Imagine a cord pulling you up – as if there's an extension to your spinal cord coming out through the crown of your head – a little like you're a puppet in the *Sound of Music*
- Lift your chin a little, but don't overstretch it
- Drop your shoulders so they're not hunched up by your ears
- Let your arms hang loosely by your side
- Keep your knees soft, so that you're ready to move when you need to
- Tilt very, very, slightly forwards so that you're full of momentum and ready for action the minute you need to be
- Keep the tension – but relax! Another of those paradoxes.

Don't think that just because you're behind a lectern or in a pulpit that your posture doesn't matter – or that clerical robes act like a cloak of invisibility. People can still see you, so you must learn how to relax. Don't pass your nerves on to us. We want to enjoy listening to you – not waste our energy feeling sorry for you.

Use the space

Next time you are in your church, shut your eyes, and try to picture in your mind the space around you. Could you describe it to someone else? Can you describe the shape of the room, the different levels within it, the arrangement of the chairs, the features, the distance between people? What are the focal points in the room? Which seats have reduced visibility?

Now, open your eyes and look at it afresh. Here are some questions you could ask yourself:

- Why has the space been organised in this way? What are the benefits?
- And what are the constraints? How can you get round those constraints?
- How can you make the most of the space you've got in order to give a sense of place or direction?
- Can you use height or depth, length or breadth to make the story come to life? Can you identify the different locations in the story? Imagine you could see your footprints afterwards. What would they tell you?
- Can you use the space to make the abstract more concrete, e.g. by moving between two places to show two opposing arguments?
- Can you move around the space at different speeds, e.g. the disciples trudging the Emmaus road, or Mary running back with the news of the resurrection?

The space is important because preaching is 'an off-the-page and into-the-air kind of an enterprise.'[68] Whether you make use of a pulpit or a platform, or surround yourself with seats on all sides, preaching in church is similar to theatre. Both preaching and theatre 'create distance. They manage space. They enable discovery, illumination, pleasure, epiphany and – ultimately – encounter, by making room for them.'[69]

So, the use of space is at the heart of the sermon, because it gives space for thought, imagination, connection and, ultimately, faith.

For preaching team meetings or personal reflection

1. Do the standing still exercise (see above).
2. Hold your team meeting in the church. Discuss the space and how you could use it better for teaching.
3. Watch recordings of each other. Is there too much movement? Or too little?

Problems with the presentation

Complaint 9: The sermon is short of breath

What's the biggest problem with Henry Sermon's speaking skills? Bad breath – not the smell, but the bad control of breath.

Now this would be reasonable if the patient had been swinging from the gargoyles, but, alas, nothing so entertaining ever enters his head. He just doesn't take enough breath into his lungs to do the job. If you ask him to speak up, he'll argue that he doesn't want to sound as if he's shouting or hectoring people. That will put people right off. Either he's too theatrical, with a sermonising voice that sounds like John Gielgud on steroids or – more likely – he's not theatrical enough. 'I've got to be myself,' he says, 'and all that luvvy stuff is just not appropriate in church.'

So, he never raises his voice – either in pitch or volume. He just speaks into the microphone in his normal conversational way and hopes that this wonderful new-fangled bit of technology will do all the work. This is all well and good for a while, but it lacks the dynamism and energy needed for any venue that's bigger than a living room, where people are spread out, and the nearest person is forty feet away. With so little effort, the pitch of his voice never goes up. His low, slow voice gets even lower and slower, until it sinks into his boots. As a result, the snores and whistles you hear are not coming from him...

Remedies for breathlessness

If you think of the body as a car, the fuel is breath. The amount of breath you take into your lungs determines how far you can go. More breath means a longer, more interesting journey for the audience. Small intakes of breath into the lungs restrict your options, so that there's not enough power or expression to capture or keep people's attention. What people may notice when they're listening to you – that you're too quiet, too monotonous, or speaking down in your boots – has its source in the centre of the body: the lungs and diaphragm. Fragmenting your sentences too much makes it hard work for people to listen to you.

The good news is that it only takes a gulp of fresh air to change things. You've just got to keep doing it! That way people will listen better and engage with what you're saying.

Give yourself a check-up

Many people don't know how to describe their voice – they certainly don't like listening to themselves in recordings. But to help you to assess your own voice you just need to take a deep breath (!) and use the X Factor checklist (see Appendix 1, p. 146). Show the list to someone else who can tell you what you sound like. Or use the Voice Profile (see Appendix 2, p. 148). This gives you the words to describe your voice and can help you identify how to improve.

Check the ventilation system

Bad or inefficient use of breath can also affect the tone of your voice. Is your voice soft and sexy, or bold and assertive? And which do you want to sound like when you're in church?! You will probably want to sound confident, but warm and friendly, too. A breathy voice may leave your audience feeling anxious about your ability to lead. A sexy voice may lead to quiet words with the elders. (Or possibly a contract with Radio 4.)

If you intend to talk softly at any point, you will need to compensate by attacking your words more so that the vocal folds do their work, otherwise the breath leaks away to no purpose.

You can check how much breath is coming out by saying 'Ah' whilst putting your hand up in front of your mouth as you speak. When you give the vowel some attack, the sound will be harder-edged and you'll feel less breath on your hand. Alternatively, hold a mirror near your mouth and see if any condensation collects. If it does, you'll know that too much breath is escaping and the sound is being made inefficiently. Another way of checking breath control is to light a candle and see if you can speak close up to it without blowing it out.

> Don't speak in a preachy kind of way – that'll just send people to sleep and switch their brain off.

Taking the hiss out of it

Some people have too much sibilance in their voice – their words 'hiss' like when the treble is turned up too high on the hi-fi. It comes from holding on to the 's' 'sh' 'ch' 'z' 'ts' or 'j' sounds too long – the tongue and the lips get in the way. The answer is to open the jaw more and cut off the end of the sound so you finish words more cleanly.

This problem is exacerbated by hearing loss, since the sibilant spectrum occurs in the high frequency range (5-10 kHz) and you may not be aware that you are doing this. If in doubt, ask others.

Pump up the volume

A microphone can amplify your voice, but it can't give you energy, enthusiasm or passion, all of which are a crucial part of your toolbox of communication skills. This is not just about shouting – it's about dynamism, energy levels and stage presence. The person operating the soundboard can turn up the volume all they like, but it won't compensate for a lack of dynamism. Abraham Lincoln said 'When I hear a man preach, I like to see him act as if he were fighting bees.'[*]

Sometimes people preaching and reading in church use the lower end of their voice range, without enough contrast from the upper end. They do this because they are still in conversation mode, not presentation mode (and, more than likely, using a microphone). When you are relaxed, and making less effort, as you would be in normal conversation, you are likely to speak lower. Investing more energy into your voice and body will have the effect of raising the pitch. So as with projection, it all comes down to energy levels – which all comes back to breath.

Exercise your lungs

If you want to check your breath for capacity, try these exercises next time you're in the shower. You'll soon get a reaction!

1. The Light Switch Exercise

To check whether you are using your diaphragm sufficiently, put one hand, palm down, on the top of your stomach, just below the rib cage. Now, imagine at the far end of the room that there's a light switch, one that can be operated by the sound of your voice. Take a deep breath and give the commands, 'On! Off! On! Off!' Can you feel the diaphragm muscle working? Singers refer to this muscular power as 'belt'.

---

[*] If you actually did fight bees, it would make the sermon a lot more interesting.

2. Holler!

How much breath and energy will it take to fill your church? Aim to get the walls vibrating with sound – rather than leaving it to the PA and getting a load of feedback. Try saying the excerpt below. Take a deep breath first and be ready to give it all you've got (only don't breathe out before you start – that'll just hurt your throat).

> *A voice from off shouts, 'Holler!'*
> *Isaiah calls back, 'Just tell me what and I'll shout the house*
> *down.'*[70]

3. Speak Up! Then Down

To work on varying the tone, practise saying 'Oh no!' Take a deep breath and give it some welly. Now try it high, then low, then in between. Now try the same with 'Whoo hoo!'

Slow down, you speak too fast!

Some people go so fast they barely pause for breath. Others, in an effort to be clear and emphatic, go too slowly. The sermon limps along to a conclusion, but not before the audience has expired. If someone tells you you're going too fast, there are three remedies:

1. Look up

Establish eye contact with your audience, and prolong the eye contact so that you are checking whether people are with you or not, especially if the concepts are profound or complex. If you are asking rhetorical questions, give people sufficient time, in their minds, to begin to articulate an answer. This gives you time to draw breath.

2. Speak more loudly

This will require you to take more breath and will force you to slow down, articulate more clearly and give the consonants more attack. It will also wake up the people on the back row.

3. Move about

Not purposelessly like a headless chicken, but with a sense of direction. Using the space purposefully forces you to pace yourself more and to slow up at points. For instance, in telling the story of the Good Samaritan, you can demonstrate the road where the band of robbers beat up their victim. You might walk from Jerusalem, on your left, to Jericho, on your right. This introduces a natural pause into your endless flow, as well as helping people to visualise the story. Now it's true that sometimes you will want to talk as you walk, but take the opportunity sometimes to give it a break!

Speed up

> Avoid the monotones.

What if you go too slow? People might not recognise the opposite condition as slow delivery. They will probably tell you that you are clear (and maybe measured) – what they might not say is that it sounds dull. When you are practising your sermon, just for fun, try doubling the speed at which you speak. It will force you to take more breath and give life to both you and your sermon, making you more energetic and full of zest. (Another way of doing this is to inhale helium before the sermon – but this will make you sound like Pinky and Perky, so we don't recommend it.)[*]

For preaching team meetings or personal reflection

1. Use the X Factor Checklist or Voice Profile (see p. 146).

2. Invite someone with experience in voice production to give you some training.

3. Plan a session at church with someone who runs the PA. Practise being loud and energetic, both with and without a microphone.

---

[*] For more information on voice production, see http://www.singwise.com

Now what?

Some of you might have read the diagnosis of the state of the sermon, and felt that it doesn't go far enough. In your church the sermon doesn't need a bit of gentle treatment, it needs major surgery.

You might feel that we haven't really addressed the root cause of the problem. After all, tweaking the sermon might make the preaching better, you might be holding people's attention, you might be preaching on subjects that they actually care about, but you'll still be preaching. And it's not actually making any difference to their lives.

So here's a thought: perhaps what the sermon really needs is not a load of conventional remedies. Perhaps it just needs to go away and lie down for a bit. You know, have a bit of a holiday, go and lie on a beach with a pile of books and a bottle of sun tan lotion. Get some colour back into its little homiletic cheeks.

Just because 'The Lord is the same yesterday today and forever', doesn't mean that the teaching methods have to be.

If you're thinking like that, then maybe it's time to consider alternative therapies: approaches that some would consider unorthodox, but that might still achieve the goal of making Christian disciples.

HENRY SERMON 'GOES INTO REHAB'

Revered communicator books into wacko clinic

Henry Sermon has left hospital and gone into a rehab clinic. Doctors hope that alternative therapy could succeed where conventional medicine has failed.

According to hospital sources, his doctors are right behind the treatment.

'We felt he needed a complete rest,' they said. 'We didn't want to pump him full of drugs – we tried that in the sixties and it didn't work. (Although a lot of his listeners said his sermons actually made more sense under the influence of hallucinogens.) We tried giving him steroids, but he ended up giving Matron a forty-five minute lecture on eschatology yesterday. She said that if he does that again, she'll kick him right up the apocalypse.'

Doctors are hopeful that a complete break will help.

'It can't do any harm,' said a Doctor. 'I say give him some time off, send him on holiday. Let him have fun. After all, they say laughter is the best medicine. Although I think you could make quite a good case for penicillin.'

Henry, pictured at a meditation session at his rehab clinic.

'It might just work'

Speaking from his newly-installed flotation tank in the University of Badenbaden-wurtemflugenstaffenberg, Professor Heinz von Beanztin told us 'It's totally crazy, man, but it just might work.'

The Professor wants Henry to get back to his roots. 'After all, this was once a hip guy. I mean, look at the communicators in the Bible, they taught in some crazy ways. It was all "Once upon a time" and "Here have some honey and locusts" and "Taking all their clothes off". Not that I'm suggesting the latter for Henry. That wouldn't be therapeutic for anyone.'

New approach to life

It is not certain how long Henry intends to be in rehab, or if he intends to ditch his old style completely and embrace a totally new approach to life. He has checked into the establishment known as the Rectory.

'It's a bit like the Priory, only more Anglican,' explained the owner, the Very Enlightened Juniper Clearwater.

'Henry Sermon's employers have been working him hard every week, twice a week, for hundreds of years now,' she continued. 'He needs to get out of church. I mean, 1850 years old and he's never had a gap year. Give the guy some space.'

Part Three

Alternative Therapies

Have you lost your faith in mainstream medicine? Have you tried tweaking the speaking, but nothing's changed? Then maybe you need some alternative therapies.

This section is all about radical alternatives to the twenty minute monologue. These approaches are about:

- changing the culture in church
- changing the relationship between people
- reducing the predictability of the message
- giving people more of a voice
- encouraging more mature learning
- allowing more independent thinking
- and, most of all, moving people away from passive obedience to considered, committed and creative discipleship of Jesus Christ.

Does this mean banning sermons forever?[*] No, we're not suggesting that. We haven't lost confidence in the power of the spoken word, nor the written word of the Bible, nor the Divine Wordman, Jesus – to transform. We have confidence in the sermon as a means to enthuse, rally, inspire, inform and testify. But we're also challenged by the way Jesus grew disciples. And we think there is a missing link – between the sermon and the maturing disciple. Something is not connecting between the two.

The sermon isn't the be-all and end-all of the church service and it's time we stopped treating it that way. People don't come to church to worship the sermon, the preacher or the Bible – and if they do, it's time they stopped. People don't come to Christ because they desperately need to hear a sermon every week. They come to Christ because he can change

---

* There's a thought. Never mind 'Back to Church Sunday' – maybe 'No Sermon Sunday' would bring people flooding back.

them and change the world. They come to him for his healing power, for forgiveness and peace with God, for life to the max!

Jesus was a speaker and story-teller, an activist, performance-prophet, a miracle worker. If all we do each week is just sit his followers down and make them listen, we are reducing discipleship to a matter of sitting still. It's a bit like joining a gym, only to find that each time you visit, you are sat down in the corner and given a lecture about physical fitness. And then, on top of that, you're told to go away and do your exercise at home.

Let's get the focus right. 'Be doers of the word, and not merely hearers who deceive themselves' warns James (James 1:22). Our worship is towards God, our Creator, Redeemer and Guide. Our meetings are supposed to equip people to be active followers, not to suck the life out of them. Our teaching and training can take whatever form it likes – as long as people learn. It's OK to give the sermon a rest. God will give life and resurrection where He wants and wills.

Risky learning

The ideas in this section involve letting people participate in the learning and draw their own conclusions. This approach is, by its very nature, risky, and in the church, generally we don't like risky learning. Churches obsessed with doctrinal purity don't like the idea of people Getting It Wrong.

But really, all these methods do is legitimise what is already happening in the pews. People are already drawing their own conclusions and coming up with their own ideas. It's just that, in the normal service structure, there's no place for those ideas to be expressed. Too many preachers mistake the congregation's silence for agreement. But it might just be politeness. Or disbelief. Or a coma.

> We have to open up. People are reluctant to do that, but if we don't, then we're not really going to grow.

Jesus allowed people the liberty to Get it Wrong. He told open-ended stories, he scattered riddles and provocations, like unexploded bombs. Risky learning has its dangers, but at least it is never in danger of being forgettable.

A bit about the learning process...

And we should remember that, even with a traditional structure, the sermon is only a part of the learning process – maybe a quarter. According to Dave Meier, there are four stages to the learning process: preparation, presentation, practice and performance.

- **Preparation** refers to anything you do to make people eager to learn: sending out fliers before a sermon series, or giving people biblical examples of holy living at the start of a service. It also is the stage at which you aim to get rid of any obstacles to learning, e.g. the thoughts that this is going to be boring or a waste of time.
- **Presentation** is when the content of the learning material is delivered, either aurally or visually, or both.
- **Practice** gives people a chance to try out their new knowledge or skills or understanding, there and then.
- **Performance** is where people independently practise what has been preached, because they've assimilated the new learning into their lives.

We can see that the sermon sits squarely in the presentation stage, but the crucial thing is that *people will only get the most out of the sermon if the rest of the phases take place, too.* Meier describes how all four phases have to work together to achieve maximum effect.

- If the **preparation** phase is weak, people will have no motivation to learn
- If the **presentation** phase is weak, there's no encounter with the subject matter
- If the **practice** phase is weak, the learning does not even begin to get integrated into people's lives
- If the **performance** phase is weak, there's no application – and the whole process has been a waste of time![71]

The problem with the traditional sermon is that, even when the presentation phase is OK – the sermon itself – often the other three phases are either weak or missing entirely.

If we are really serious about teaching in the church – as opposed to standing and talking – then the other phases are crucial. This means turning ourselves into teachers as well as speakers, and broadening our communication skills to include the visual as well as the verbal. Or, if we can't do those things, we must share the teaching process with others. This is because...

It's not all about you

The minute you open your mouth, it'll be obvious what you are bringing to the party, but what's everyone else bringing to church, in terms of experience, knowledge, values and skills?

> I would like to see a follow up to sermons for people who are having difficulties. I don't believe asking people to come forward for prayer helps every time. In my own experience, after listening to motivating, God-inspired sermons, I found that where I responded and was expecting God to help me with my various troubles, it didn't happen, and I still had the same problems years later. It was only when I decided to do something about them that change took place. So, what I am saying is, preaching should be followed up by some kind of ministry to help people work through their personal issues. Any type of call to action should have a follow up plan.

In 1983, David Kolb, an American education theorist, wrote *Experiential Learning: Experience as the Source of Learning and Development* in which he proposed a cyclical model of learning. In this cycle, people move from Experience, to Reflection, to Conceptualising, to Action and then back round to Experience. Kolb shows how people learn from reflecting on experience, and encourages teachers to use that as a core part of their teaching.[72]

This approach has had a huge effect on the education world. It revolutionised teaching and training in both education and business. So it comes as no surprise to realise that the church has taken hardly any notice of it whatsoever.

> Share actual experiences.

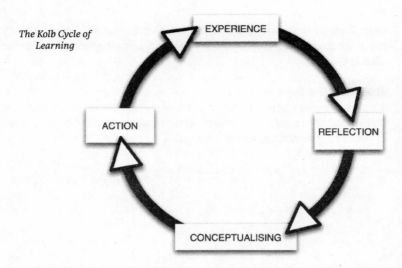

The Kolb Cycle of Learning

The sermon barely even acknowledges people's experience, never mind reflecting on it. Through anecdote, it usually tries to second-guess the congregation's experience, but as for really *knowing* it and using it as starting point for learning, it's hardly begun. Phrases like, 'I don't know about you, but ...' can irritate our audience when we plough on regardless, as if we don't really want to know. People need the chance to articulate and reflect on what they're learning Monday to Saturday and although lots of churches have midweek homegroups that could assist the process, frequently the sermons and homegroups exist as two different worlds – roughly in the same orbit, but rarely communicating. Small groups give a forum for sharing experience, but they're just not focused enough to sharpen thought or stimulate action. What discussion questions there are, are usually designed to make sure that, whatever happens, people get the point. So you get questions where the answer is so mind-numbingly obvious that it could only be missed by people with the IQ of a plank.

   'Was Jesus (a) a good man? Or (b) a bad man?'

Allow times of sharing from the front to show how God has been working in individual lives today, i.e. Testimony Time.

As with all theories, Kolb's theory is not without its critics, and we may rightly be wary of seeing it as the only way to plan our teaching. Nevertheless, the value of people's experience as part of the learning process needs to be considered. How far have we come from the way Jesus taught his disciples, or proclaimed the kingdom to others? How much of that was reliant on sermons? And how much was conducted through practical experience? Christ engaged people and brought them into God's kingdom through moving and doing, observing and picturing, problem-solving and reflecting, as well as talking and hearing.

The previous section of this book was largely about the way the preacher talks and does the teaching. In this section, the big difference is that each approach allows people to talk – the one thing that sermons (and sometimes whole services) rarely make room for.

Group Therapy

Include more people in the preaching plan.

As we've seen, the sermon has its roots in conversation, and some churches are taking this seriously. The conversation continues through the week through collaborative preaching. It's an alternative therapy for the sermon that gives the preacher a chance to step down from their 'sovereign' position in order to listen to the listeners.

'Learning is difficult when the church overstresses the individual' says Margaret Cooling. 'We learn best in relationships. When people know and respect each other, they are more willing to listen to what others have to say, whether in informal groups or in more formal teaching and preaching situations.'[73] This agrees with the observation of Edwin H. Friedman, ordained rabbi, family therapist and author

> *Communication does not depend on syntax, or eloquence, or rhetoric, or articulation but on the emotional context in which the message is being heard. People can only hear you when they are moving toward you, and they are not likely to when your words are pursuing them. Even the choicest words lose their power when they are used to overpower. Attitudes are the real figures of speech.*[74]

Through changing the status levels in church, collaborative preaching can change the people's attitudes to learning. The goal is deep engagement by all: everyone motivated by the process – everyone motivated to become like Christ. In this model, the Sunday service still includes a sermon, but it takes a different place in the process of the body of Christ learning together. Although a few clergy had begun to try this approach in various pockets of the Church from the sixties onwards, in 1995, when John McClure wrote *The Roundtable Pulpit*, it was, and still is, a radical alternative to the norm.[75]

In practical terms, he suggests that to preach collaboratively you need a sermon brainstorming group – no larger than ten – hosted by a preacher, that meets once a week for a maximum of an hour and a half. The aim for the discussion is to help the church interact with the Bible, and come to terms with what the gospel requires of Christians. It's a chance to offer insights into interpretation, to contribute to the planning process, to review the previous week and to feed into the coming week. For those who require it, he offers some sharp questions for discussion.

Obviously the group is only a small percentage of the congregation, so how does the rest of the church get involved? McClure encourages a regular change of membership to the group – say, every quarter – staggering the change so that there is always a stable core. Those who aren't a part of the group can provide feedback. And of course, with the internet, this is even easier now – a possibility which McClure foresaw in 1995.[76]

Of course, collaboration can take different forms. Here, a student at Wycliffe Hall cites a slightly different model

> *At my old church the ministry team met for an hour each week on the Thursday morning before the Sunday service to let the preacher talk through what they thought God was saying through the passage and to let them share what they were going to preach on. Once they had shared for fifteen minutes the rest of the staff were able to chip in comments and ideas. I didn't actually preach there but I think most of the preachers found it a really helpful exercise. Sometimes comments from the meeting would completely change the angle of approach the preacher took, or showed that they'd really misunderstood the thrust of the passage. Those were helpful things for the preachers.*

This can be combined with the ideas about feedback (see p. 81) but it's important to note that this is a proactive process. The idea is to help you shape a sermon that is coming up, not reflect on one that's just been delivered.

Widen the group

> Leaders and ministers seem to have a secret society.

These examples show ministers consulting their staff about what and how to preach. This is good practice, but it still restricts the input to the 'professionals', as it were. The ministry team will likely be very good on theology and pretty good on technique, but will they ask the same questions of your sermon as the person in the pew? Moreover, what signals is it giving out when only the 'officials' are consulted? It could simply reinforce the hierarchical view of preaching, where an elite few get to have their say.

The value of extending this process beyond the ministry team or the elders to all and sundry is that the whole dynamic of the teaching in church is changed. Jonny Baker, National Youth Co-ordinator in the UK for the Church Mission Society, makes an impassioned plea for teamwork

> *Stop being a lone ranger. Don't do all the preaching. Get in a team of people that want to communicate and dream ideas and creative ways of communicating – and widen that group as much as you can.*[77]

Widening the group can also mean sharing the actual teaching itself. One of the preaching team at our church told us of an example he saw on a visit to another church

> *Three of the congregation were contributing. The first gave a short introduction on the opening six verses of James. The second (the minister) gave the central focus for twenty minutes with a handout*

for the congregation to make notes on. The third person presented the ten minute conclusion which was very practical and talked about current experience.

Increasingly, people live and work in collaborative environments. They work together on documents where each suggestion and change can be tracked. They expect to have a collaborative input. To carry on excluding the listeners from shaping the preaching of the church will, increasingly, be anachronistic.

*Common Surfship**

There is no reason why, if people bring laptops into the sermon space, that they shouldn't be used. This doesn't mean you have people surfing the web while you are preaching.** But it could be that they look up information during the question and answer phase, or even after the service. Ask people to find the answers for themselves. They can search commentaries, discover the significance of the Greek (or Hebrew), look at maps for significant places, distances, journeys.

When you want to draw people back, give them clear instructions so that the focus is where you want it to be. Here's where preachers need to learn from teachers. A core teaching skill is the ability to get your classroom to stop what they're doing and listen. And preachers may well need to do the same thing. It's best to be really clear and straightforward. Make sure people put down their laptops/blackberries/notebooks and give their attention back to you before you carry on speaking. A gentle way of making the transition between research or group time and plenary time might be to mention in advance that you will give a musical or visual cue. 'When you hear the music start up/when you see a picture appear on the screen ... that's the time to put down your laptops so we can carry on talking about ...'. You might ask people to note down the most important thing they've discovered, or share it with the person sitting next to them, or shut their eyes and think it through, before you proceed.

Collaboration is here. Best ride the wave before it rolls over you.

---

* Claire is responsible for these puns. I just want to make that clear. And for those of a nervous disposition be warned: there are even worse ones on the way.

** Actually they might be doing this. They might be playing Tetris or Patience. But, the fact is, with or without computers, people can always find other things to do if they're bored.

Casting Pods

Having more than one speaker gives you several different perspectives on a biblical passage or theological issue. It makes speech less formal, less dogmatic, with possibly more colour and shade of opinion. If your church doesn't give people the opportunity for this, there are podcasts that do. Godpod, for example, produced by St Paul's Theological Centre, gives the listener a chance to hear three people discussing a topic, plus guests on specialist subjects.[78]

Some churches, like businesses, can be very protective of their teaching product and may not alert people to other ways of learning like this, but we need to be inspiring and encouraging people to take every opportunity to learn and grow. Let's not assume that the only way to hear God's word is on a Sunday morning in church.

The unfinished sermon

> It would be nice to have dynamic talks – with visuals, sound, props, etc – but also with the opportunity to ask questions and challenge the speaker if appropriate.

We want to make a case for the incomplete sermon.

Many preachers write their sermons out in full – wasting far too much time agonising about their choice of words. If you were to read last Sunday's sermon, the chances are it would be a well-crafted piece of text, complete in itself. But people don't come to church to read, but to respond. They come because church offers a place to worship, pray, to work through the challenge of living for Christ in today's world. If that were not true, you could just publish your sermon, hand it out as people arrive.

> Allow more group discussion and Bible study – different groups for different levels.

Nevertheless, the sermon is frequently viewed as a discrete set piece. Even when it is integrated thematically with the songs and the prayers, it is generally considered to begin when the preacher stands up and to end when they sit down. But that shouldn't be the end of it. The end of the sermon should not be the end of the learning. Sermons should be open-ended.

As we've said already, that means giving people the right of reply. The teaching is incomplete without it.

Give time for questions after the sermon.

Get us to talk about what we've heard in the sermon as part of the service.

The right to reply

A change of culture is necessary. People will only be ready to talk back to the sermon when you give them the permission to do so. So how do we make that happen? Here's your chance to think that through.

So, get your pen out and fill in the blanks. You have our permission!*

1. The apostle Paul, as we know, taught people through his letters, letters which we are very happy to read out in church. But, as we have seen, he also taught people through dialogue and debate – why don't we do that?

---

* Assuming that you own this book. If you've borrowed it from a library don't fill in the blanks. And if you've borrowed it from a friend, go out and buy your own copy. We need the money.

2. The simplest way to give people the right of reply would be to invite them to ask questions at the end of the sermon. This is common practice in just about any setting where someone speaks in public – but it is strangely rare in churches. Why?

3. Some would argue that all you'd get is shared, collective ignorance; others have suggested that you might discover the people in the pews have a wisdom and experience that can make the learning richer. What do you think?

4. The average size of congregation in the UK is 84 (in Anglican churches, it's 54).[79] Some churches, however, are much bigger than that, others a lot smaller. How does the size of the congregation affect its ability to discuss and debate?

And a few final quickies:
- What is the size of your church?
- Is it possible to know everybody's names?
- What kind of interaction is possible for that number of people?

Interactive learning can and should happen in preaching. Get people to engage with each other before/during/after the sermon – it wakes them up to the issues. But I don't want the learning process to be derailed by unhelpful, inconsequential random chats!

The thing is, if your congregation numbers around twenty to forty or less, you're only around the size of an average class at school, or two classes at most. In that context, dialogue would be expected. Not only that, one-to-one mentoring is definitely possible, too.

There's nothing new about this, either. In an article on interactive preaching, Stuart Murray tells us that sixteenth century Anabaptists moved away from the monologue tradition toward a more interactive style of teaching, with multiple participation and dialogue.[80] He quotes Ambrosius Spitelmaier, an Anabaptist in 1527, who explained – under interrogation – how this worked

> When they have come together, they teach one another the divine Word and one asks the other: how do you understand this saying? Thus there is among them a diligent living according to the divine Word.

Drama Therapy

> *Use more drama.*

I dream of a church where interaction is possible, where reply is permissible, where learning is irresistible. I dream of a place that I call 'forum church'.

Being a drama teacher, I'm inspired by theatre as much as by theology, and 'forum church' would, for me, be a happy fusion of the two. Does that mean a spotlight on the preacher and liturgical dancing girls? No.[*] Of course the word 'theatre' might suggest a proscenium stage, a big red curtain, lights, tiered seating, two dimensional sets and a lot of people calling each other 'darling', but those are just the accessories. In the same way, when you mention 'church' to someone, what may first come to mind is a pulpit, pews, a hushed silence and a lot of people calling each other 'dearly beloved', but as we know, this is not the only model of church.

The model: forum theatre

In 'forum theatre', you might have none of the above accessories, but you would have the essentials: actors and an audience. Instead of a stage, you might find the performance in a shanty town among the favelas, no curtain protecting the world of make believe, no clever lighting or other tricks, just actors showing scenes to an audience. In forum theatre, once the actors have demonstrated a scene, the audience are invited to comment on the way characters behave. They become 'spect-actors' who might even be invited to step into the actor's shoes, and replay the scene again, reacting as they might. It's theatre, but not as we know it.

Augusto Boal, a theatre director who died in 2009, pioneered 'forum theatre' and modelled it as a way of empowering people to bring about change in their neighbourhood. He was also a city councillor in Rio de Janeiro from 1993-96, where he used this process to give people the chance to promulgate new laws – laws to do with hospitals and crèches, laws that would benefit the blind and the mentally ill. He did all this through

---

[*] Shame.

theatre, pushing the verb 'to act' as far as it would go. In the last few years, Boal's approach has inspired theatre groups and others around the world to empower people who've previously had no voice.[*] That's what can happen when you breathe new life into old forms, when you encourage dialogue rather than monologue. People become energised and make a difference to their society.

How would you do it?

So what would 'forum church' look like? To literally follow Boal's model doesn't depend on having great actors and writers in your midst – although if you have, this would give them a great outlet for their skills. It doesn't necessarily need scripts, rehearsals, performances. It needs a willingness to get people involved with the teaching matter, discussing how to follow Christ and make a difference to society. You just need to be ready to give people a picture of how things are and how they might be.

Let me give an example. Let's say you want to encourage people to pray about their work. You might start with a Bible passage on prayer, or with one of Jesus' parables, or with a video that shows how missionaries use their work to reach others for Christ. Whatever you do to introduce the subject, you want the congregation to put themselves in the picture. So you create a tableau that will plant the idea in their minds and will stay with them all week.

- Stage 1: You ask people to think about their work environment. You get everyone to turn to someone sitting near them and mime what they do when they're working (the other person can guess what it is!) Alternatively, they can describe what they do at work. If you prefer, ask a few people to show what they do: a waitress cleaning a table, a surgeon performing an operation, a mother changing a nappy – forewarn them if necessary.

- Stage 2: After a few seconds ask them to 'freeze' – so that you get a snapshot, as if you were taking a photo of them at work. Ask the person up front, or those watching the mime, when they pray about work. They might say: first thing in the morning, in the middle of what they're doing, or on their way home. They might confess that prayer doesn't happen at all.

---

[*] You can find out more at http://www.theatreoftheoppressed.org

> Make a clear connection between the
> illustrations and the teaching/thinking
> points.

- Stage 3: Seize the moment for prayer there and then. Ask the person up front, or the congregation, to pray for their work and all those affected by their work. Create a physical picture for this: shutting eyes, lifting a document to God, placing a hand on someone's shoulder. Ask them what they would say. Ask others for suggestions for how to pray. Or offer your own suggestion for prayer. They can do this silently, or in pairs, or with a written prayer – however you like – but the point is, don't just talk about it, do it. Turn your listeners into learners: there and then.

- Stage 4: Lastly, and this is most important, encourage people to repeat the process, *in situ*, when they're not in church, using these suggestions during the week.

And the next week, report back on it. Don't lob this idea into the ether, never to return. Keep the forum open.

Once you're feeling confident with the approach, you might even try it outside! In front of the church, in the market square, by a stone cross (which is where preaching used to take place), or a signpost somewhere – wherever people gather, engage them in the drama of debate.

Shock-ratic Therapy*

Have you heard of Socratic questioning? No? You've never used this method of disciplined questioning, to pursue thought, tease out ideas and open up issues and problems? If I said that anyone interested in teaching at a deeper level should start by learning how to ask good questions, would you agree?

When you are reading the Bible, do you find you have questions? What do you do with those questions? How do you feel as you grapple with those questions? How does your church feel about questions? Does it encourage questioning? In what settings?

---

* I did try to warn you about the puns.

When you preach, do you ask questions? Or do you just give answers? If you ask questions, do you let people answer them? Are you happy to let people call out in church? Or is polite silence the usual expectation of your congregation?

Do you let other people ask you questions? Or would that put you off your stride? Can you answer their questions? Is it your job to be able to answer all their questions?

What do questions do? Yes, what *do* questions do?

Do they help you ascertain what people already know? Do they help you discover what people understand? Do they help you find out what people actually do? Or are they just annoying when you get too many?

Are all questions good? What would make a question bad? Do you generally ask closed questions that elicit a 'Yes' or a 'No'? Well, do you? Or would you know how to ask an open question?

Have you heard of Socrates? Who was he? What did he do? How did he do it? What's the easiest way of finding out how people have trialled his teaching method today?

Can you think of anybody in the Bible who asked people questions to further their understanding of God?

Was there anybody who let other people ask them questions to further their understanding of God?

How has the Church used this approach in the past? Are there other ways to use questions?

How could you use questions next time you want people to learn? How would it make a difference to you? And to others?

Speech Therapy
Another way to get 'sermons' surfing beyond the Church's four walls is to encourage the congregation to take them to new places, and do it for themselves. Jonny Baker records his experience

> *One of the things I realised several years ago was that I had a lot of friends who had been Christians a while and were drifting out of churches. Sermons were the thing they most complained about. I know that for me one of the times I got the most out of the Bible was when I had a sermon to prepare because it made me study it in-depth. I figured that these people needed to do something like*

that. So I started a group called 'nuggets'. We met in a pub and everyone had to deliver a 'nugget' (as well as drink plenty of beer). Now a nugget was an insight on a passage in the Bible – it could be anything. But being a competitive bunch, people wanted to deliver impressive nuggets. The unspoken thing was that the more original and surprising the better. And a good nugget generally had a build-up, the delivery and then basking in the oohs and aahs as people were wowed by it. This was the most fantastic time of learning for the whole group – the group had shifted from being passive bored listeners to active producers – learning and making discoveries in the process. The one qualified theologian in the group actually invariably delivered the best nugget and I think he enjoyed it so much more than preaching.[81]

The last statement is very interesting, for clearly what Jonny Baker calls 'nuggets' are essentially small sermons by another name.

Elsewhere, a vicar realised that the sermon was not engaging with a group of men in his church, and simply took them out for a discussion in a local coffee shop during the sermon slot while someone else preached to those who remained. Making people active rather than passive learners revitalises the art of preaching and hugely engages people in growing as disciples and as communicators.

Play Therapy

The big difference between education in schools today and, say, forty years ago, is that there's a lot more active learning these days. When I trained as a teacher twenty years ago, I pretty soon learned to keep the teacher talk to a minimum. Education wasn't about me telling the class facts or impressing them with my skills, it was about them discovering knowledge, skills and even values. And from the student's point of view, that's far more fun. When the brain sees learning as fun, it ignores distractions and sticks around for more.

This is true wherever we are. If we could become like children in church, I believe we would learn a lot more, and worship more freely. Unfortunately, we often dismiss a whole raft of possible ways of teaching because we are too concerned to appeal to the 'adult' side of the congregation. C. S. Lewis relates that, at ten years old, he read fairy tales in secret. As a man, he was no longer gripped by the fear of childishness and read them openly.

If we free ourselves from the fear of needing to sound grown-up in church, we'll open ourselves up to a whole new realm of fantastic resources: poems, puzzles, quizzes, stories, drama, games, making stuff. We can learn through these things as much as children can. And, whisper it low, but many of us would rather like the opportunity. I wonder how many people in church look on with silent envy as the children leave for what are often called 'their classes'? How many of us secretly wish that, instead of staying in and listening to the twenty-minute monologue, we were going out to draw, or watch a video, or create a scale-model replica of the ark of the covenant out of Lego? All it takes is the willingness to let go.

> Use action.

Takeover Day

For the last couple of years at our church we've had Takeover Sunday (a church response to the annual national initiative 'Takeover Day' that takes place in November). The idea was that, for one day, the children would be in charge; the normal hierarchy would be reversed. And so the children did the music, led the service, and even preached the sermon.

One year, at the point where the children usually leave, it was the adults who got up, left the church building and crossed to the hall. There, they were offered a choice of activities. They could do some art, they could join the 'boffins' in the kitchen, using commentaries and study Bibles to look at a passage, they could do some drama out in the garden. The interesting thing was the dynamic atmosphere and the gusto with which people threw themselves into it. This was not a token gesture – it was real learning.

Resources that have been produced with children in mind can be adapted to stretch adults' teaching. Even if the knowledge assumption is pitched too low for your congregation, you can still use the approach.

Karl Barth can be taught through a limerick.* New Testament Greek can be taught through puppets.

The point is that it's the teacher's research, study, knowledge and understanding, and the way that they use different media for learning, that opens up the possibilities. Look at the success of the Horrible Histories series – both the writing and on TV: the authors know exactly how to make their knowledge digestible. The result is that people learn things – and enjoy learning them. Many emerging churches are rediscovering the playful aspect of celebration, with kite-flying at Pentecost and painting during worship.

'Playful preachers do not overemphasize exegetical data,' suggests Richard Hansen

> As a young preacher, I was certain that if I marshalled enough exegetical evidence (from the original languages, of course), I could bludgeon my listeners into belief. My sermons were like boxing matches: I didn't always score a knockout, but I expected to win on points. Since then, I have joined the Mohammed Ali school of homiletics. I must learn to dance like a butterfly if I want to sting like a bee. The footwork of the sermon (how you say it) is just as, if not more, essential than the content (what you say). [82]

Creative Bible study

Why should All Age services have all the best ideas? What's sauce for the goose is sauce for the gander. Margaret Cooling's book *Creating a Learning Church* shows how learning can take place with very little emphasis on 'teacher talk'. 'We learn best,' she says 'when we *use* information and engage with it' (my italics). She gives many different examples of how this can be done – all of which are frequently used in school settings, but which in fact meet the holistic needs of worshippers just as well.

> *Think about the Sunday club. They may be able to repeat the story*

---

* E.g.,   Reading the works of Karl Barth,
            Should never be done for a laugh.
            At 4,000 pages
            Church Dogmatics takes ages,
            And if you piled all the volumes on top of each other they'd be about as tall as a giraffe.
            (OK, I admit it still needs a bit of work...)

of David and Goliath, but can they use it in their lives? We may be
able to repeat various texts and beliefs, but have they become a
part of us? It is important for our lives as Christians that Scripture
does become a part of us.[83]

Her suggestions for working with a Bible passage include the
following:

- taking your senses for a walk (ask what you would see, hear, taste, touch, smell)
- highlighting the verbs
- finding the emotions
- looking for speech and thought
- discovering images
- finding an important decision
- turning the passage into some kind of prayer

All these things would get people to actively engage with the Bible,
with the preacher barely saying a word. And it's as easy to do this in a
large meeting as in a small group. If you want to stretch people a bit more,
however, she gives plenty of other ideas, e.g. writing lyrics, using different
drama approaches, creating a ritual or designing a DVD cover, all of which
require people to interact with the text, with all their heart and soul and
strength and mind.[84] These approaches are particularly useful for those
who are very familiar with the Bible, for whom it has lost its sparkle and
fizz.

Godly Play

Godly Play is an approach used by some churches with their children's
groups. It uses play as a starting point and wonder as a catalyst for learning.
Its creator, Dr Rebecca Nye, says

The heart of Godly Play is that it does not depend on knowledge, but
on personal response and spiritual engagement with God's word
within a supportive, safe community of friends. Consequently it
'works' with all ages, including adults, and it works well in groups
with a wide age or ability range. It began as an approach for very

*young children – aged 3-6. However, it lends itself to the most
sophisticated theological reflection too; I use it with ordinands …
increasingly those working with adults are finding it has such deep
potential to reach people directly, simply, 'where they are'.*[85]

She describes how her three year old daughter continued to 'play her
own way' with the character of the Good Shepherd, at home. 'A long
bedtime ritual was played out as the Good Shepherd tucked in and kissed
each sheep – showing limitless patience when certain (all too familiar)
sheep wanted an extra kiss, a glass of water or a light left on. Finally, they
were all safely asleep. She placed the Good Shepherd at the entrance to
the sheepfold, looked at the scene she'd created saying 'Oh, the Good
Shepherd might be lonely now. He does wish the sheep could wake up
sometimes and love him back.'

Through play, her young daughter reached a spiritual insight. There's
no reason why adults shouldn't do the same. Yes, we're always glad when
given a chance to sit down, but one of the discoveries of recent research
on how to get the most out of people learning, focuses on the need to
move, to get up and do. For some reason, the church accepts that this is
what children need, and we produce the most amazing resources to help
them do it – but do we do this for adults? When the adult teaching begins
in church we ask everyone to sit down – only getting up to stretch our legs
when a hymn comes along. Over the road where the children's teaching
takes place, we ask them to get up. And if we didn't ask them, some of
them would do it anyway!

A Roamer Therapy*

It's not just children who need to get up and move. Some people get itchy
feet if they sit down indoors for too long. If you want to keep them with
you, why not take the sermon for a walk? You'll be in good company:
some of the most eminent preachers down the ages have been outdoor
preachers. Whitefield and Wesley, Spurgeon, Moody, Carey, William and
Catherine Booth – as well as preaching in churches, they walked the streets
or preached in fields. How many of us, as preachers would be prepared to
do that? Would we cope?

---

* I can't take it any more…

Come on, join in at
the back!

GREAT MOMENTS IN PREACHING
No.8 – WHITEFIELD INVENTS THE MEXICAN WAVE

When John Wesley was refused permission to preach in St Andrews, Epworth, Lincolnshire, the church of his childhood, his answer was that he would preach from the only free piece of land near by. He climbed on top of his father's grave, six foot away from the church door, and preached 'You must be born again.' Said Wesley, 'I am well assured that I did far more good to my Lincolnshire parishioners by preaching three days on my father's tomb than I did by preaching three years in his pulpit.' In addition he said, 'To this day, field preaching is a cross to me, but I know my commission and see no other way of preaching the gospel to every creature.'

It was outdoor preaching which was to make Wesley's younger contemporary, George Whitefield, famous. In Bristol, he went out to the collieries of nearby Kingswood and decided to preach to the miners right there. That week, two hundred miners heard him. A week later, five thousand came to listen. Two days after that, ten thousand were in the crowd. Soon it had doubled again, to twenty thousand. Later still, back in London, he preached to a crowd estimated at eighty thousand.

Francis of Assisi was not afraid to take his message to the people, 'sometimes preaching in up to five villages a day, often outdoors. In the country, Francis often spoke from a bale of straw or a granary doorway. In town, he would climb on a box or up steps in a public building. ... He apparently was a bit of a showman. He imitated the troubadours, employing poetry and word pictures to drive the message home. When he described the Nativity, listeners felt as if Mary was giving birth before their eyes; in rehearsing the crucifixion, the crowd (as did Francis) would shed tears.'[86]

Francis is also credited with creating the original 'living nativity' in 1223-4. Inspired by local shepherds, he is supposed to have taken people to a cave outside the small Italian town of Greccio. There they saw a re-enactment of the nativity scene, with people dressed in biblical robes, a manger and real animals. Some churches have followed his example at Christmas, to tell people the story of Jesus' birth. There's no reason why it shouldn't be used to convey other messages at other times of the year, too.[87]

Jerusaleynsham

We sometimes associate street preaching with a very aggressive form of evangelism. But does it have to be this way? Especially if you're English! It doesn't have to be. Getting out of doors can be a great way of reaching a different audience, bringing the Bible alive in new places, whilst at the same time getting people walking and talking about Jesus.

We live in Eynsham, near Oxford, and roughly three years ago, in preparation for Easter, we decided we wanted to tell the story of Holy Week – but with a difference. We wanted a Holy Week that would help people imaginatively engage with the times and the places, the people and the events – a Holy Week that would actually prepare you for Good Friday and Easter Sunday. We wanted to relive the events of Christ's last week on earth and we thought this would appeal to other people, too, but we couldn't afford to take everyone to Jerusalem. So we decided to bring Jerusalem to us. Jerusaleynsham was born.

We took an online map of Ancient Jerusalem and an online map of Eynsham and put one on top of the other. Rather spookily, we discovered the boundaries were almost the same! This allowed us to roughly locate the key places in the gospel accounts. The playing fields become the Temple complex; the nearby village of Cassington became Bethany; Golgotha –

the site of the crucifixion – was situated in the car park. We met each day, morning and evening, to read the appropriate portions of the Bible and to hear them put in context. And we moved between locations.

At the end of the week, early on Easter Sunday morning, Mary (well Carole, actually) ran from the Garden of Gethsemane (well, the public toilets) down an alleyway, past the chemist's, down Station Road, to fetch Peter and John (well, Robin and Dave). They all arrived back, about fifteen minutes later, puffing and panting, as we read the account of the resurrection.

Of course, this can take place anywhere – you just need to translate the key principles of time and place into your own setting (see Nick's website for more details).*

Art Therapy

Have you ever been to an art exhibition, a display, or an installation? Can you remember what you saw? What effect did it have on you?

Those of us who love words, and are convinced of the power they exert (whether written or spoken) may have never really considered the impact the visual can have. Yet, ask an artist. Ask someone in advertising. Ask someone in video production whether people take any notice of images. Do we watch television more than listening to radio? If the answer is yes, then our own habits are telling us how important the visual can be. Do we learn anything from pictures? Well, think what a difference it would make if they were taken away.

People learn by observing and picturing. And some churches have realised this. Some churches realised this centuries ago. But aside from some cathedrals and the odd stained glass window, these days, many churches almost have a blindspot to the arts. Their church walls and furniture may be decorated with images from another era, and it's as if no-one sees them any more – they've been filtered out. To put up new images amongst them, or in place of them, would seem offensive to some. Or perhaps certain forms would be acceptable, for instance banners or kneelers, whereas sculpture or abstract art would not. If you were to paint the whitewashed walls of your medieval thousand year old church, today,

---

* It's now called 'The Longest Week Live'. More information on www.nickpage.co.uk. We've already taken it to Jerusalymington. It's best if you live in a place beginning with 'l' or a vowel! Perhaps one day it will become Jerusaliverpool. Or Jerusalondon.

with brightly coloured pictures, in the manner of medieval wall paintings, would people be shocked?

One way round this would be to put on a temporary exhibition. It needn't be so threatening – even as temporary as for one hour a week – and could be very stimulating. Could it achieve more than a twenty minute sermon? Well, maybe, just maybe – pound for pound – it might.

There are other ways of getting visuals up there. You could use a data projector – or ordinary slide projector – to put images on the walls. You could have an image printed on vinyl (kind of like a post-modern church banner). You could have a big TV in the corner, or a tiny, digital frame, displaying a succession of images.

Curates or Curators?

Sadly, churches have been a place of frustration rather than fervour for the artistically inclined. In some cases people have left to form alternative places of worship that give them the space to express their creativity. On the positive side, this has led to some fresh and innovative forms of church. Ambient Wonder, for instance, in Norwich, uses the terminology of an art gallery to describe its group meetings. For each event one person takes on the role of 'curator'; their role is to draw together the contributions of others and create the space for those who come to encounter God.

On the negative side, it is a loss to the mainstream churches when this creative input seeps away. This is how Kester Brewin reflects on what led him to plant Vaux, an alternative worship group, in London

> *Sitting in pews; standing up; sitting down; the same format each week. It just wasn't working for us ... We were frustrated. We sat each week surrounded by some of the brightest talents in film, TV, theatre, art, social work and politics who were made to watch in virtual silence because they didn't play guitar and didn't preach. These were the only two gifts that were acceptable as worship. It just seemed such a waste.*[88]

Greenbelt Christian Arts Festival in the UK, however, has given groups such as Sanctum, from Horsham, the opportunity to demonstrate 'Christian worship done differently.' Describing themselves as people 'having fun providing spaces that help people communicate in creative ways with God', Sanctum's early tagline was 'No singing, No sermon, Never mind.' Finding new ways of encouraging learning amidst the worship experience does not mean that the emerging church eschews 'speaching' (as Doug Pagitt would call it).[89] It just takes a different place. fEAST, an alternative worship group in Hackney, East London, meets weekly, but might only have a speaker one week out of four: other weeks are centred round creative liturgy and discussion.

Such approaches provide different stimuli to learning and for that many people will be grateful, but by themselves they won't necessarily lead to disciplined Christians, any more than a sermon will. That's why it's good to be aware of how these approaches contribute to the learning cycle, whether the preparation, presentation, practice or performance phase.

> *Be more creative with the order of the worship service.*

Another group, Ikon, in Belfast, gives people plenty to look at as well as to listen to. So, for instance, if you were to enter one of their meetings, you might find yourself in a bar, filled with the smell of burning incense. A DJ is mixing the words *Eloi, eloi, lama sabacthani* into the music, while an artist is writing the English translation 'My God, My God, why have you forsaken me?' in black paint on to a canvas. Holbein's picture of 'The Dead Christ in the Tomb' is projected behind the stage. A man talks (as he drinks) with the music in the background and the artist's work taking shape. A woman continues the thought. Someone else's words segue into a song on guitar. Someone lifts a candle and speaks about the 'Tenebrae' service, blowing the candles out at the end. The projected view of Christ melts into darkness. Another speaker describes a dream. In the darkness, yet another speaker helps people to visualise a meeting with God – will they follow Christ regardless of heaven or hell? There is no formal end to the meeting but gradually people begin to open their eyes and talk. As candles are re-lit and the music starts up again, everyone is given a candle and a burnt match as a reminder of the experience.[*]

---

[*] It sounds uncannily like our church business meetings.

Says the leader, Peter Rollins, 'the evangelical nature of the community does not resemble a one-way diatribe leading from "us" to "them" but rather embodies a multiple dialogue that moves from one to another.'[90] So although there is no one sermon, you could say there are lots of small sermonettes. Insights on the Holy Saturday experience are shared by various men and women – but no one person does all the talking. Is there a leader? Who can tell?

Mixing it up

Steve Taylor runs a church in Opawa, New Zealand. Like a DJ, he melds art, poetry, and DVD clips from films and commercials with Scripture, to create a unique sampling – reflecting 21st century Christianity and culture. For instance, in his website, he describes using images of balloons to inspire liturgy after going to the see the film *Up*.

The church runs a monthly prayer service called 'Soak' that combines sung worship for about thirty minutes, *lectio divina* for about fifteen minutes, and various stations for communion, confession and journalling. All this in a church beautifully lit with candles and draped with fabric, creating what he calls 'a very rich space'. On a night when the theme is 'Hearing God in sickness', he tells us, one of the stations is a wheelchair where people can sit and pray for those they know who are sick. Another station offers healing prayer, others offer 'poetic and tactile' prayers for those hearing difficult news. People can leave when they feel they've finished 'soaking', through doors with a benediction taped to them.

'Soak' has no sermon, but Taylor insists it is a challenging space where 'the Bible has been liberated, allowed to become a springboard for prayer rather than something to analytically dissect.' It offers, 'what I, for lack of a better word, am calling an adult space. So much church spoon feeds you. Every minute is programmed and full. You are not required to do much. In contrast, at Soak, if you lack an inner world and don't want to work that inner world, you get bored pretty quick.'[91]

Have you prepared yourself spiritually? Are you soaked in prayer before you speak?

Those who are suspicious of such creativity fear that the Bible gets lost in translation, but as Doug McConnell testifies in his foreword to Taylor's book *The Out of Bounds Church*, 'One of the great strengths of Steve's contribution comes out of his insistence on "extreme discipleship" rather than "Christianity lite".'[92] And it has results, says Taylor – people regularly stay for over two hours, visitors ask for baptism, even teenage boys love it.

Holistic learning

With the kind of services described above, it's difficult to say where prayer and worship end and learning begins – you just can't see the join. But then learning to know God can't be contained in a sermon. As Margaret Cooling says

> *Learning in the Bible means far more than learning facts. 'Yada', the Hebrew word that is often translated 'know' covers factual knowledge but also means close personal experience and encounter. 'Yada' is not just knowledge about God; it is knowledge of God. It goes beyond information to meaning, beyond facts to understanding and experience that changes our lives.*

Too often, church sees 'learning' as the act of stuffing our heads with information. Cooling argues that people need to be helped to find meaning in the Bible, to discover new ways to see God

> *We cannot assume that this will just happen. Whenever we split learning into several parts (information, meaning, application) we reduce our ability to learn. Discovering meaning and applying it to our lives helps us to learn information because we tend to remember what we put into practice, so we should think of the different levels of learning as woven together rather than as separate threads.*[93]

Steve Taylor's view is that 'The church has trained one muscle well – that of the Bible speaker. In so doing, we have lost the muscles of community learning. It will take a while to recover those muscles. There will be some inevitable ups and downs as we re-learn. Which makes it such an exciting time to be Bible people today.'[94]

I have two pleas. To those who are rigorously scriptural, I would say: give room for people to participate and learn creatively. To those who are rigorously creative: give room for the Scriptures to be learned and digested. That way we would see the kingdom of Christ extended through orthodoxy and innovation.

Narrative Therapy

If you're wanting more creative ideas, take a look at Matt Madden's *99 Ways to Tell a Story* – a series of one-page comics that uses a minimal plotline in a variety of ways.[95] Madden was inspired by Raymond Queneau's *Exercises in Style*, which tells a simple story in 99 different styles and genres.[96]

Is it possible to do the same with the Bible? Why not set yourself the challenge! I offer a list below to get you started. They might be things you would do yourself to find a new way into the Bible. Or they might be activities for you to get other people doing in church meetings, home groups, youth groups, or in cafe style services where you have tables. The aim is to drive people back to the text to see what the Bible really says, and how it's put together. The possibilities are endless!

(Theological Health Warning: Of course this involves playing around with the content and form of the original Bible text – so if you can't go with that, as a concept, you had better skip this page.)

- **Change the viewpoint**
  First, identify the viewpoint that the text is written from. Is it first person, e.g., 'I was cupbearer to the king'? Or third person 'He was the king's cupbearer'? Try writing it out from a different point of view. You could explore the perspectives of unnamed, very peripheral, people mentioned in text. You could even tell the story from the point of view of an animal, or an inanimate object, e.g., Jonah's story from the point of view of the big fish or the shady plant!

- **Change the setting**
  Place the story somewhere else in the world. Or take it to several different places: move round the globe from East to West, or North to South, or from one continent to another.

- **Change the tense**
  Try changing a Bible passage that's in the past tense, e.g. 'Two days ago there was a wedding in Cana' to the present, 'There's this

wedding in Cana happening today' or even the future, 'There's going to be a wedding in Cana tomorrow.'

- **Action following**
  Explore what will happen the next day after the events have occurred, say the day after Jesus' ascension.

- **Action preceding**
  Explore what was happening the day before the events occurred, say the day before Palm Sunday.

- **Change the genre**
  Imitate a really recognisable iconic form: e.g., a well-known film or television programme, as you tell the story eg Dr Who lands on Noah's Ark, Sylvester Stallone plays Goliath.

- **Turn it into a diagram**
  A map, a timeline, a flow diagram – these are all familiar forms, but be more inventive if you want. Find pictorial ways of describing the relationships between characters or ideas through spider diagrams or your own original mind maps (for examples see http://en.Wikipedia.org/wiki/Mind_maps).

> *Give us illustrations, examples, the 'how to'.*

- **Turn it into instructions**
  For instance, from the miracle of Jesus' healing of a deaf man, extrapolate 'How to Heal a Deaf Man.'

- **Add characters**
  Include present day characters – even people who are well-known to your church! This is a device that Renaissance artists used: they would include people from the present in pictures of the past.

- **Sketch a storyboard**
  Fold a piece of A4 paper in half, then half again, then half again. Drawing stick figures, break the narrative down into a series of eight scenes, as if for a film, and sketch one in each box – with a caption.

- **Create a picture poem**
  Use actual lines from the text if you like, but reshape them to make a picture. For instance, write out the words of Psalm 1 in the shape of a tree.

- **Get close-up**
  Describe the action from close-up – notice the detail of the face, fingers or key objects, the action, the emotion.
- **Distance yourself**
  Describe the landscape or the action from a distance. How far away can you get? For instance, 'The angels looked down from heaven and saw a man, woman and a donkey, trudging along a dusty road.'
- **Describe opposites**
  Create the 'anti-passage'. What would the opposite of the Bible text be?
- **Change the order**
  Print out the text. Cut it into chunks or sentences. Randomly re-sequence it. Or experiment with the palindromic model, i.e. the first sentence becomes the last and the sentences are read in reverse order. Then ask people to sequence it correctly. This is good for establishing the order of a narrative or the logic of an argument. With some texts the order may be less important, e.g. Proverbs or Psalms. Re-sequence on a different basis, e.g. the most important proverbs for fathers.

Preaching As a Subversive Activity

Neil Postman and Charles Weingartner wrote *Teaching as a Subversive Activity* for American schools in 1969. But many of their insights are as fresh as the day they wrote them and could possibly help us in the church in the 21st century. Towards the end of the book, there is a chapter entitled 'So What Do You Do Now?'[97] And its questions are as sharp as ever. We have reworked them here for the benefit of those who teach and train Christians.

Subversive preaching: some suggested approaches

1. Write at the top of your sermon notes: 'What am I going to have Jesus' followers do today? What's it good for? How do I know?'
2. Prepare a series of sessions giving no answers, just giving people a problem to work through with the Bible at hand and God as their guide. 'Don't be worried by silence' say the authors. (Most of us preachers probably won't feel daunted by that.)

3. When asking questions, try to listen to people's answers and hold back from commenting. Ask another person to make notes, so that we can talk together afterwards about the response. A dispassionate observer may be better placed to analyse what was said and suggest the next step.

4. Ask people to list questions in response to a passage of the Bible, or encourage them to talk only in questions. Give problems such as: 'Suppose we wanted to make people the best possible disciples we could imagine, what would we need to know in order to proceed?'

5. Allow people to surprise you with their knowledge and wisdom. We can hold people back by having low expectations, or by not giving them space to think for themselves.

6. Imagine that your congregation were the most amazing followers of Jesus! Imagine they have the greatest (not the least) potential for putting God's words into practice. What would you do differently? (Of course, this might mean accepting that they know and can do stuff you can't even manage.)

7. Try this experiment – tell your church that God has forgiven them and will be welcoming them into heaven. Ask 'What do you now need to live the rest of your lives?'

8. Shift the focus away from the past and ask future-oriented questions. The authors' example, though devised for school over forty years ago, would still be relevant to us in church today: 'What effects on our society do you think the following technological inventions will have?' Postman and Weingartner go on to give as examples: cars, phones, TV, planes, central data storage. You might update this to cover the internet, video-conferencing, the e-book, whatever's new. This is a perfectly valid kind of question for Christians to be asking themselves.[98]

> Interact with people – with more handouts, for example.

Dave Walker's CartoonChurch website has some brilliant – and brilliantly funny – worksheets. The *Church of the Future* worksheet would be perfect for this occasion.

It's equally possible to ask other kinds of questions about Christians and society. For instance, 'What effect would we see on our society if:

a) everyone believed in God

b) everyone was a follower of Jesus Christ

c) everyone here practised forgiveness to everyone, all the time?'

Of course, it's not enough just to lob the question out into the ether. You've got to hear the answers, and encourage a way forward.

Shifting the focus to the future doesn't mean you don't look back at the past in your attempt to come up with some solutions. You can bring the two together. You could, for instance, read or rewrite Acts 2:43-47, but change 'the apostles' to the name of your church. What would not ring true? What could justifiably be added? How does that help you forge a way forward as a church?

9. Look at the effect of the media on attitudes to Jesus, the Bible, church. How is it influencing people? Don't think that you've got to become an expert on *Eastenders* or Twitter in order to be able to lead this kind of session. That's exactly where other people's observations will be so valuable.

The authors of *Teaching as a Subversive Activity* end their book with words that we would want to echo

> *There is nothing in what we have said in this book that precludes the use, at one time or another, of any of the conventional methods and materials of learning ... What we are asking for is a methodological and psychological shift in emphasis in the roles of teacher and student, a fundamental change in the nature of the classroom environment ... It is neither required nor desirable that everything about one's performance as a teacher be changed. Just the most important things.*[99]

HENRY SERMON IS BACK
Doctors hail miracle cure

Doctors are reporting that Henry Sermon has made a miraculous recovery. One doctor described the 1850 year old as being 'fit as a fiddle, although why anyone has ever thought a violin fit is beyond me.'

'It was touch and go for a while there,' said Professor Heinz von Beanztin, newly-appointed Dean of the University of Badenbadenwurtemflugenstaffenberg. 'But he's a remarkable old creature. If there's one thing he's demonstrated across the centuries, it's an ability to reinvent himself.'

'It really is amazing,' said his (former) therapist, Dr Larry Pepper. 'He phoned me up this morning and sacked me. Said he'd been taking himself far too seriously and it was time to cut loose and have a bit of fun.'

Following his spell in hospital, Henry has been spotted at many churches across the country.

Unrecognisable

'We didn't recognise him at first,' said one churchgoer. 'He looked completely different. He came in and started asking us all these questions. It was only at the end we realised that he'd been there at all.'

'I didn't like it at first,' said churchgoer Major-General Doris Bracegirdle (Retd). 'I'd just settled down for my usual snooze when he popped up beside me and asked what I thought about the issue. I don't think I've ever been asked that in church before. In the end it was quite invigorating. Mind you, I drew the line when he got the crayons out. And then I drew a circle as well.'

Since then Henry has been seen in pubs and cafés, at shopping arcades and car boot sales.

'It's not so surprising when you think about it,' countered Prof Von Beanztin. 'After all, he's in the business of resurrection. And, although he might have got stuck in a rut in the past, it's not like he hasn't taken chances before. Whether on the hillsides of Galilee, small churches in fourth century north Africa, Lincolnshire graveyards, the Surrey Music Hall, the Whalemens' chapel in Boston – whenever he comes to life again miracles happen.'

The Professor stopped and raised a glass.

'At this rate,' he said, 'he could go on for years.'

Henry Sermon, in the best shape of his life.

Prescription

Keep taking the tablets

We wrote this book because we wanted things to change. We're not claiming that the book contains a miracle cure, nor are we, by any means, the first people to point out that something is rotten in the state of preaching.

In the States and the UK, in the last thirty years or so, many preachers and teachers have written books recommending new and exciting directions for taking the sermon – so why has so little changed? Why has Henry's condition not improved? Is he, as we suggested at the beginning, incurable? Or is he simply not taking the tablets?

There are many reasons why the sermon continues to struggle. Partly it's because local preachers and even ministerial students are simply not told what treatments are available. The books remain stuffed away, in the obscure recesses of the homiletics section in the college library, where nobody ever goes.

Partly it's because returning anybody to fitness takes time. These solutions are not, for the most part, quick fixes. Some of them you may be able to implement quickly, and all of them will make a difference, but none are an instant miracle cure. It's like going to the gym. You don't – alas – walk in there as a wimp and come out twenty minutes later as a warrior. It takes time to turn Charles Hawtrey into Charles Atlas.

Mainly, though, it's because none of the solutions are easy. They all require varying degrees of effort. The solutions we've suggested involve things like listening to others, taking direction and advice, opening oneself up to criticism. They mean searching out new materials and learning new techniques.

This is, in fact, one of the main reasons why the sermon has survived for so long: because it's easy.

We don't mean that it's easy to do. We mean, practically, in terms of preparation and resources, it's the simplest form of teaching possible. One person, one set of notes, that's all it takes. The monologue sermon is ubiquitous because it is the least demanding way of communicating a message. An unaccompanied monologue requires no liaison or consultation with other people. You don't have to think up discussion questions or work out interesting visuals. You just do your prep, write your notes, drag yourself to the lectern and away you go. In terms of preparation, the sermon is easy.

By now a lot of preachers will be harrumphing like mad.[*] 'Sermon preparation easy?' Well, perhaps 'easy' is the wrong word. Perhaps 'straightforward' is better. But compared to more collaborative, interactive approaches, sitting in your study and deciding what you are going to say is much easier.

The fact is, that if your preaching is going to change, it's going to take effort. It's not going to be easy to get your homiletic six-pack back. But we hope that our suggestions, either for remedies or alternative approaches, will help.

Don't consign them to the wastebasket or flush them down the loo. Try them. Continue taking them, three times a day, if necessary.

And if the symptoms persist, consult a bishop.

Why am I a preacher?

In *Teaching as a Subversive Activity,* the authors' final, final question is 'Why am I a teacher, anyway?' And it is just as vital for those who presume to stand up in front of others at church to ask: 'Why am I a preacher?'

This, really, is what lies at the heart of this book. Why do we preach? Is it because we love the feeling of power? Or because we like being the centre of attention? Maybe we have a strong sense of calling but, if so, what is the proof of that calling? Do we preach because it's expected of us, part of the job? Or because we long to see people understand more of the Bible, more of what it means to be a disciple, more of God?

---

[*] Actually, many of them probably started 'harrumphing' around page 6.

For sure, none of us are doing it for the money. We might get a bit of a thrill about having a congregation listen to us – although preachers who have the highest view of preaching can be the humblest men or women – but that's not really it. We preach because we want people to change their minds and lives. We preach because we want people to become active, energetic, empowered, fruitful citizens of the kingdom of God.

Why am I a preacher? Finding an honest answer to that question will set us free. It might set us free to do things differently, or not to preach the sermon at all. It might set us free to explore radical ways of teaching: to spend time with those people we are trying to teach. It may give us the freedom to give up preaching altogether. We need to respond to what's happening around us. Society has changed and is changing still. The old relationships have been swept away by technology, by today's culture, by the media. Old ways of teaching have disappeared from our schools and universities and it is inevitable that the church, too, will be affected.

This is not something to fear. If anything, it takes the church back to its roots. It takes us back to a time when homilies and sermons were *homileo* and *sermo* – conversations rather than lectures. It takes us back to small, smokelit rooms in Troas, to the shade of olive trees overlooking Jerusalem, to a group of disciples talking and learning and discovering what it was to follow Christ.

Why am I a preacher?

If it is not to serve the Church, then I had better shut up.

Appendix

appendix /əˈpen.dɪks/

n. a small tube-shaped organ, which joins the intestines on the right side of the body. In humans it has no use.

Here, in the appendix, we come to the small tube-shaped part that is joined to the right side of the book. However, it could be very useful in preparing sermons. There are three resources here for the teachable speaker: the *X Factor Checklist*, the *Voice Profile*, and *Remember: Voice Matters*, giving you some helpful vocabulary to describe your voice and manner, and a few reminders before getting up to speak.

Of course, if it feels too painful and causes you to grumble, it may indicate that you have an infection – but remember, you can always have it removed.

APPENDIX 1: THE X FACTOR
Listen to the person speak and answer these questions.

Projection
- Is X easily heard?
- Is their voice vibrant, dynamic, powerful?
- Or is it too quiet? Or too flat?
- Do they use contrast or is the volume all at one level?
- Is the breath used efficiently? Or do they seem too breathy?

Articulation
- Is their voice clear and crisp?
- Or do they mumble?
- Are they too tense (tight jaw) or too relaxed (lazy lips)?
- Or are certain sounds being misplaced (eg 'r's or 's's)?

Pitch
- Is their voice interesting, with variety of expression?
- Or is it predominantly too low, down in their boots (could be a sign of not enough energy or zest)?

- Or too high (could be a sign of speaking from the neck, with lack of breath from diaphragm)?
- Is it bright and resonant? (If not, they need to smile, and open their jaw more)

Pace

- Are they fluent and well-paced?
- Or are they too slow and measured?
- Too fast to hear words, or follow content?
- Are they hesitant, too many ums and ers?
- Do they use pause and silence effectively?

The human touch

- Are they warm and friendly or cool and clinical?
- Natural or strained?
- Passionate and enthusiastic or lacking in energy?
- Do they look people in the eye?

Movement

- Do they rely on a full script for sermons? Or do they use notes?
- Have they got a strategy for gradually coming off the text?
- Are they able to move about?
- Do they use movement with freedom, purpose and confidence?
- Do they use direction and pace to enhance what they are saying?
- Or are they just edging about uncertainly or pacing about aimlessly?
- Are they wooden when gesturing or moving?
- Are they comfortable with telling or acting out stories, conveying character, using humour?

Helping people learn

- Are they showing an awareness of what makes people listen?
- Are they thinking through what helps people learn?
- Are they considering the different needs of those in the congregation?
- Are they comfortable interacting with people, e.g. encouraging purposeful discussion, using questions and answers as part of the learning process?

APPENDIX 2: *Voice Profile*
Listen to the speaker and mark them on the scale from 1 to 5.

NEGATIVE	1	2	3	4	5	POSITIVE
VOLUME						
Too quiet	1	2	3	4	5	Good projection, easily heard
Flat	1	2	3	4	5	Vibrant, dynamic, powerful
ARTICULATION						
Slushy	1	2	3	4	5	Clear
Lazy lips	1	2	3	4	5	Crisp
Tangled tongue	1	2	3	4	5	Controlled
Tight jaw	1	2	3	4	5	Open mouth
Mumbling	1	2	3	4	5	Projection
Mispronunciation	1	2	3	4	5	Good pronunciation
PACE						
Fragmented	1	2	3	4	5	Smooth
Too slow/ too fast	1	2	3	4	5	Fluent
Unvaried	1	2	3	4	5	Varied
Hesitant	1	2	3	4	5	Deliberate
VOICE QUALITY						
Nasal	1	2	3	4	5	Open
Breathy	1	2	3	4	5	Efficient use of breath
Harsh	1	2	3	4	5	Mellow
Lifeless	1	2	3	4	5	Enthusiastic
Emotionless	1	2	3	4	5	Conveys emotion
Unfriendly	1	2	3	4	5	Warm, friendly
Strained	1	2	3	4	5	Natural
Monotonous	1	2	3	4	5	Varied expression

APPENDIX 3: A CHECKLIST

Copy this out and stick it somewhere useful! You could keep it on the fridge, or as a bookmark, or put it in the vestry and go through it before the service begins. (You can download a copy from the 43rd Point website.)

Remember! (voice matters)

Stand tall
Look at your listeners
Smile
Breathe deeply
Fill your lungs with air
Open your mouth wide
And power your words
Invest them with energy
Work your mouth muscles
Your tongue and your lips
Your teeth and your jaw
Turn up the volume!
Then reduce it to a whisper
Sometimes look away, turn your back, be silent
Explore the highs and lows of your voice
Slow, slow, quick, quick, slow
Use your eyes to draw attention
Move with freedom and purpose
A triangle of footprints
Right and left, then width, then depth
Change place, pace, space, face, voice –
and show that you're alive!
Get to know your students
as well as your Bible
Beyond their smiles,
what are they saying to you?
Beyond your words,
what are you saying to them?

Suggested Reading

Transforming the Sermon

Allen, Ronald J., *Patterns of Preaching: A Sermon Sampler* (St. Louis: Chalice Press, 1998)

Baker, Jonny, *Transforming Preaching: Communicating God's Word in a Postmodern World* (Cambridge: Grove Books, 2009)

Chadwick, Charles and Phillip Tovey, *Developing Reflective Practice for Preachers* (Cambridge: Grove Books, 2001)

Buechner, Frederick, *Telling the Truth* (New York: HarperCollins, 1975)

Childers, Jana, *Performing the Word: Preaching as Theatre* (Nashville: Abingdon Press, 1999)

Edwards, J. Kent, *Effective First-Person Biblical Preaching: The Steps From Text to Narrative Sermon* (Grand Rapids: Zondervan, 2005)

Florence, Anna Carter, 'The Preaching Imagination' in Thomas G. Long and Leonora Tubbs Tisdale (eds), *Teaching Preaching as a Christian Practice: A New Approach to Homiletical Pedagogy* (Louisville: Westminster/John Knox Press, 2008)

Littledale, Richard, *Stale Bread? A Handbook for Speaking the Story* (Edinburgh: Saint Andrew Press, 2007)

McClure, John S., *The Roundtable Pulpit: Where Leadership and Preaching Meet* (Nashville: Abingdon Press, 1995)

Pagitt, Doug, *Preaching Re-Imagined: The Role of the Sermon in Communities of Faith* (Zondervan, 2005)

Stevenson, Geoffrey, *Pulpit Journeys* (London: Darton, Longman and Todd, 2006)

Taylor, Steve, *The Out of Bounds Church? Learning to Create a Community of Faith in a Culture of Change* (Grand Rapids: Zondervan, 2005)

How People Learn

Cooling, Margaret, *Creating a Learning Church: Improving Teaching and Learning in the Local Church* (Oxford: Bible Reading Fellowship, 2005)

Mathews, Alice, *Preaching That Speaks to Women* (Grand Rapids: Baker Academic, 2003)

Meier, Dave, *The Accelerated Learning Handbook: A Creative Guide to Designing and Delivering Faster, More Effective Training Programs* (New York: McGraw-Hill Professional, 2000)

Postman, Neil and Charles Weingartner, *Teaching as a Subversive Activity* (New York: Delta, 1971)

History of Preaching

Dargan, Edwin C. and Ralph G. Turnbull, *A History of Preaching* (Grand Rapids: Baker Book House, 1974)

Edwards, O. C., *A History of Preaching* (Nashville, TN: Abingdon Press, 2004)

Old, Hughes Oliphant, *The Reading and Preaching of the Scriptures in the Worship of the Christian Church* (Grand Rapids/Cambridge: W.B. Eerdmans, 1998)

Kienzle, Beverly Mayne and Pamela J. Walker, *Women Preachers and Prophets Through Two Millennia of Christianity* (Berkeley: University of California Press, 1998)

Wilson, Paul Scott, *A Concise History of Preaching* (Nashville: Abingdon Press, 1992)

Modern Communication

Hipps, Shane, *Flickering Pixels: How Technology Shapes Your Faith* (Grand Rapids: Zondervan, 2009)

Jamieson, Kathleen Hall, *Eloquence in an Electronic Age: The Transformation of Political Speechmaking* (New York: OUP USA, 1988)

Larson, Craig Brian and Haddon W. Robinson, *The Art and Craft of Biblical Preaching: A Comprehensive Resource for Today's Communicators* (Grand Rapids: Zondervan, 2005)

Creativity, Voice Production and General Luvviness

Barkworth, Peter, *About Acting* (London: Martin Secker & Warburg Ltd, 1980)

Madden, Matt, *99 Ways to Tell a Story* (London: Jonathan Cape Ltd, 2006)

Queneau, Raymond, *Exercises in Style* (Oneworld Classics Ltd, 2008)

Tharp, Twyla and Mark Reiter, *The Creative Habit: Learn it and Use it for Life: A Practical Guide* (New York: Simon & Schuster, 2006)

Pressfield, Steven, *The War of Art: Break Through the Blocks and Win Your Inner Creative Battles* (New York: Warner Books, 2003)

NOTES

Preliminary Diagnosis

1   Augustine, *Essential Sermons* (New York: New City Press: 2007), 17–18.
2   Craddock, Fred B., *As One Without Authority* (St. Louis: Chalice Press, 2001), 21.

Part 1 Medical History

3   Old, Hughes Oliphant, *The Reading and Preaching of the Scriptures in the Worship of the Christian Church* (Grand Rapids; Cambridge: W.B. Eerdmans, 1998), I, 7.
4   Stott, John R. W., *I Believe in Preaching* (London: Hodder & Stoughton, 1982), 15.
5   Old, *The Reading and Preaching of the Scriptures in the Worship of the Christian Church*, 49.
6   See for example Ezekiel 3:22-6:14; Jeremiah 13, 27-28; Isaiah 20:2-4.
7   1 Kings 11:27-32.
8   Acts 21:11-12.
9   See 'Language of the Prophets' in *The Anchor Bible Dictionary*, ed. David Noel Freedman (New York: Doubleday, 1999), V, 482–89.
10 Thornton, John F. and Katharine Washburn, *The Times Greatest Sermons of the Last 2000 Years : Tongues of Angels, Tongues of Men* (London: HarperCollins, 1999), 9.
11 Nolland, John, *Luke* (Dallas: Word Books, 1989), 194.
12 *Sirach* 51.23.
13 Safrai, Shemuel and M. Stern, *The Jewish People in the First Century: Historical Geography, Political History, Social, Cultural and Religious Life and Institutions* (Crint: Van Gorcum, 1974), II, 935.
14 On Synagogue worship see Daniel-Rops, Henri and Patrick O'Brian, *Daily Life in Palestine At the Time of Christ* (London: Weidenfeld and Nicolson, 1962), 371–76.
15 Bailey, Kenneth E., *Jesus Through Middle Eastern Eyes: Cultural Studies in the Gospels* (London: SPCK, 2008), 147.
16 Bailey, *Jesus Through Middle Eastern Eyes*, 151.
17 M. Megillah 4.4 in Danby, Herbert, *The Mishnah, Translated From the Hebrew* (London: Oxford University Press, 1933), 206.
18 Thornton and Washburn, *The Times Greatest Sermons of the Last 2000 Years* (London: HarperCollins, 1999), 7.
19 Old, *The Reading and Preaching of the Scriptures in the Worship of the Christian Church*, 108–09.
20 Old, *The Reading and Preaching of the Scriptures in the Worship of the Christian Church*, 121.
21 See Matthew 13:10-17.
22 See 'διδάσκω' in *New International Dictionary of New Testament Theology*, ed. Colin Brown (Exeter: Paternoster, 1986).

23　Mark 1:39; Matthew 9:35.

24　Dodd, C. H., *The Apostolic Preaching and Its Developments* (London: Hodder & Stoughton, 1944), 7–8.

25　Old, *The Reading and Preaching of the Scriptures in the Worship of the Christian Church*, 198.

26　Dodd, *The Apostolic Preaching and Its Developments*, 7–8.

27　'It was by *kerygma*, says Paul, not by *didache* that it pleased God to save man.' Dodd, *The Apostolic Preaching and Its Developments*, 8.

28　Bruce, F. F., *The Acts of the Apostles : The Greek Text With Introduction and Commentary* (2nd ed., London: Tyndale Press, 1952), 372.

29　Acts 17:32-33; 2 Corinthians 11:6.

30　2 Corinthians 10:10.

31　See 1 Corinthians 9:5; Romans 16:7-8; 1 Peter 4:10.

32　See Flew, R. Newton, *Jesus and His Church : A Study of the Idea of the Ecclesia in the New Testament* (Carlisle: Paternoster, 1998), 159–160.

Part 2 Complaints and Remedies

33　Bainton, quoted in Stott, *I Believe in Preaching*, 23–24.

34　Alexander, James Waddell, *Thoughts on Preaching, Being Contributions to Homiletics* (New York: Charles Scribner, 1863), 15.

35　Charles Silvester Horne, *The Romance of Preaching*. Quoted in Stott, *I Believe in Preaching*, 39.

36　Craddock, *As One Without Authority*, 5.

37　Stott, *I Believe in Preaching*, 51.

38　Buckley, Stephen, *The Prime Minister and Cabinet* (Edinburgh University Press, 2006), 100.

39　Jamieson, Kathleen Hall, *Eloquence in an Electronic Age: The Transformation of Political Speechmaking* (Oxford University Press, USA, 1988).

40　Quoted by Stuart Murray on www.interactivepreaching.net

41　Sierra, Kathy, 'Crash course in learning theory': http://headrush.typepad.com/creating_passionate_users/2006/01/crash_course_in.html

42　Florence, Anna Carter, 'The Preaching Imagination' in Long & Tisdale, *Teaching Preaching as a Christian Practice*, 123.

43　My favourite is 'The Woman Who Just Said No' by Anna Carter Florence which is told in the voice of Esther's predecessor, Queen Vashti. See at: http://day1.org/1066-the_woman_who_just_said_no. For a 'how-to' guide, see Edwards, J. Kent, *Effective First-Person Biblical Preaching: The Steps From Text to Narrative Sermon* (Grand Rapids, Zondervan, 2005) and Littledale, Richard, *Stale Bread? A Handbook for Speaking the Story* (Edinburgh: Saint Andrew Press, 2007)

44　Meier, Dave, *The Accelerated Learning Handbook: A Creative Guide to Designing and Delivering Faster, More Effective Training Programs* (New York: McGraw-Hill Professional, 2000), 48.

45　For more on their effect, see Hipps, Shane, *Flickering Pixels: How Technology Shapes Your Faith* (Grand Rapids, Zondervan, 2009).

46 Gallo, Carmine, *The Presentation Secrets of Steve Jobs: How to be Insanely Great in Front of Any Audience* (New York: McGraw-Hill Professional, 2009).

47 Quoted in Feehan, J., *Preaching in Stories* (Dublin: Mercier Press, 1989), 11.

48 Philip, William and Melvin Tinker, *The Practical Preacher: Practical Wisdom for the Pastor-Teacher* (London: Christian Focus Proclamation Trust Media, 2002), 55.

49 'The God of the Bible – The Message of the Cross, God's Choices, Not Ours', Proclamation Trust Media Sermon, 2005.

50 Quoted in Brierley, Peter, *Steps to the Future* (London: Christian Research/Scripture Union, 2000), 70.

51 Luke 19:12.

52 Luke 19:14.

53 Josephus, *Antiquities* 17.299–314; Nolland, John, *Luke* (Dallas: Word Books, 1989), 914.

54 For some interesting observations on the attitudes of listeners, see Mathews, Alice, *Preaching That Speaks to Women* (Grand Rapids: Baker Academic, 2003).

55 Genesis 22:1-24.

56 Craddock, *As One Without Authority*, 8.

57 Melville, Herman and Harold Lowther Beaver, *Moby-Dick, or, the Whale* (Harmondsworth: Penguin Books, 1972), 135.

58 Melville and Beaver, *Moby-Dick, or, the Whale*, 719.

59 Pagitt, Doug, *Preaching Re-Imagined: The Role of the Sermon in Communities of Faith* (Grand Rapids: Zondervan, 2005), 150.

60 http://www.lwpt.org.uk/preach-mainmenu-28/preaching-mainmenu-278/development.html

61 'Well-focused Preaching' in Larson, Craig Brian and Haddon W. Robinson, *The Art and Craft of Biblical Preaching: A Comprehensive Resource for Today's Communicators* (Grand Rapids: Zondervan, 2005).

62 Hill, Christopher, *Society and Puritanism in Pre-Revolutionary England* (Harmondsworth: Penguin, 1986), 56.

63 Sierra, Kathy, 'Crash course in learning theory'. Online: http://headrush.typepad.com/creating_passionate_users/2006/01/crash_course_in.html.

64 For more on Red Priest, go to http://www.piersadams.com/RedPriest/index.html

65 Webb, Joseph M., *Preaching Without Notes* (Nashville, Abingdon Press, 2001), 46

66 Cross, F. L. and Elizabeth A. Livingstone, *The Oxford Dictionary of the Christian Church* (2nd edn., Oxford: Oxford University Press, 1983), 1143.

67 Craddock, *As One Without Authority*, 14.

68 Childers, Jana, *Performing the Word: Preaching as Theatre* (Abingdon Press, 1999), 26.

69 Childers, *Performing the Word: Preaching as Theatre*, 45. For much more about the potential of movement and space, see Barkworth, Peter, *About Acting* (London: Martin Secker & Warburg Ltd, 1980)

70 Isaiah 40:6-10. From Lacey, Rob, *The Street Bible* (Grand Rapids: Zondervan, 2002).

Part 3 Alternative Therapies

71 Meier, Dave, *The Accelerated Learning Handbook* (McGraw-Hill Professional, 2000), 53–58.

72 Kolb, David A., *Experiential Learning: Experience as the Source of Learning and Development* (Englewood Cliffs ; London: Prentice-Hall, 1984).

73 Cooling, Margaret, *Creating a Learning Church: Improving Teaching and Learning in the Local Church* (Oxford: BRF, 2005), 37.

74 Friedman, Edwin H., *Friedman's Fables* (New York: Guilford Press, 1990), 5.

75 See McClure, John S., *The Roundtable Pulpit: Where Leadership and Preaching Meet* (Nashville: Abingdon Press, 1995).

76 McClure, *The Roundtable Pulpit: Where Leadership and Preaching Meet*, 108.

77 Baker, Jonny, Preaching Transformed: Communicating God's Word in a Postmodern World' (Cambridge, Grove, 2009). Based on an online article at: jonnybaker.blogs.com/ jonnybaker/text/Preaching.pdf

78 http://sptc.htb.org.uk/godpod. Doing the same kind of thing in a different kind of way, Chatter that Matters is by Steve Maltz and co at Saffron Planet (http://www.saffron-planet.net/).

79 Figures taken from the English Church Census, carried out by Christian Research on 8 May 2005.

80 http://www.interactivepreaching.net/node/29

81 From Baker, Jonny, *Transforming Preaching: Communicating God's Word in a Postmodern World* (Grove Books, 2009). The booklet is based on an article originally entitled 'Throwing a Hand Grenade in the Fruitbowl.'

82 http://www.preachingtodaysermons.com/plpr.html

83 Cooling, *Creating a Learning Church*, 80–81.

84 Cooling, *Creating a Learning Church*, 83ff.

85 http://www.godlyplay.org.uk/whatisgodlyplay.html

86 Mark Galli: http://www.christianitytoday.com/ct/2009/mayweb-only/120-42.0.htm

87 weuropeanhistory.suite101.com/article.cfm/saint_francis_of_assisi#ixzz0WMTEl5ak

88 Gibbs, Eddie and Ryan Bolger, *Emerging Churches: Creating Christian Communities in Postmodern Cultures* (SPCK Publishing, 2006), 155.

89 Pagitt, Doug, *Preaching Re-Imagined: The Role of the Sermon in Communities of Faith* (Grand Rapids, Zondervan, 2005), 48ff.

90 Rollins, Peter, *How (Not) to Speak of God* (London: SPCK, 2006), 74–5.

91 Blog item: http://www.emergentkiwi.org.nz/archive/soak-and-lectio-divina-for-those-wanting-to-hear-god-in-sickness/

92 Taylor, Steve, *The Out of Bounds Church? Learning to Create a Community of Faith in a Culture of Change* (Grand Rapids, Zondervan, 2005), 9.

93 Cooling, *Creating a Learning Church*, 23–24.

94 www.emergentkiwi.org.nz/archive/preaching-belongs-to-the-community/

95 Madden, Matt, *99 Ways to Tell a Story* (Jonathan Cape Ltd, 2006).

96 Queneau, Raymond, *Exercises in Style* (Oneworld Classics Ltd, 2008).

97 Postman, Neil and Charles Weingartner, *Teaching as a Subversive Activity* (New York: Delta, 1971), 193ff.

98 For more on this see Hipps, *Flickering Pixels: How Technology Shapes Your Faith*.

99 Postman and Weingartner, *Teaching as a Subversive Activity*, 205.

Other books by Nick and Claire Page

And now let's move into a time of nonsense

Have you ever felt frustrated with the words of worship songs? Why do they seem so meaningless?

Combining humour with strong argument, this book analyses how songwriters have bought into a disposable, 'pop-song' model. Nick Page encourages writers to really think about the lyrics of their songs and whether they are really communicating truth about God – truth which should lead to worship.

> *"Every worship leader, worship planner and Christian songwriter ought to read this book. It'll make you laugh and wince, but most importantly inspire you to think intelligently and creatively about our worship culture."*
> ***Graham Kendrick***

Celebrations and Family – All Age Worship

Two books of ready-to-use resources for all-age worship services. Using a wide range of innovative teaching activities, users will be able to simply and easily put on family services full of drama, poetry, prayers, activity ideas and lots of humour.

Drawing on many years of experience of leading all-age services, each book contains eight user-friendly, 'roadworthy' services, packed with incident and insight and all enlivened by the trademark Page humour.

Celebrations covered: New Year, Palm Sunday, Good Friday, Easter, Pentecost, Harvest, Advent, Christmas.

Family topics covered: Mums, Dads, Friends, Siblings, Money, Work, Conflict, Household Chores.